MW01222726

Spir

Awakening
A SELF-HELP GUIDE

SYLVIA KNELL

CONTENTS

INTRODUCTION

I have been working with the Spirit World all my life, and when I was two years old, my Mother passed to Spirit, but I always knew she was around me. At five years old, I used to communicate and see my Mother, and naturally, to me, I thought this was quite normal.

As I progressed through my school years, I learnt that this was not the case, and so I kept my conversations to myself. As I matured, and gradually became introduced to my Spirit Guides, it would be fair to say, that although learning mainstream schooling like many others, I was also spiritually guided by my Mum and my Spirit Friends.

I started working professionally around the age of 21 years old, and throughout my life and experiences, my spiritual family have always been there. I have never felt alone.

As I look back throughout my career, I am pleased to know that with my guides and helpers, we have been able to help many people with their Spiritual Understanding, as well as to heal their lives through the guidance, and Unconditional love from Spirit.

It seems to me that in today's society, and posts on social media, there are many people, searching for answers to their spiritual pathway and so I hope to share my knowledge and experiences, in this book, as well as spiritual wisdom from my guides, for you to perhaps find answers to some of your questions revolving around your journey.

CHAPTER 1 THE BEGINNING

There are many of us, born to the earth today, who could probably be called Spiritual Seekers. Spiritual Seeker is a term referring to someone who has some level of knowledge, within themselves, that there is a spirituality that is needing to be recognised.

Throughout the ages, Churches and Religions have tried to fill this need in each of us, to teach us to live a certain way, think a certain way, to satisfy or even perhaps save our very souls, according to their perspective born from the understandings of the teachings of the ancient texts and their subsequent interpretation of the words.

However, as the churches and religions started to grow and expand, using more and more man-made laws, eventually over time, the words of the spirit, started to become contorted and misinterpreted, and somewhere along the line, violence and fears, became uppermost and the real message of divine love to all, became lost.

Religions spun off into many different factions, and instead of preaching the words of the Divine, which is love, peace, harmony and compassion, it began to create fear, segregation and disharmony, thus leading to violence and wars.

As we look at our history books, there have been many wars, and acts of violence, in the name of religion and the divine force, which seem borne out of man's need to gain power, rather than the divinity within. Sadly, this school of thought has not changed much. Unfortunately, we are still witnessing violence and wars as man's power struggles continue. Death and destruction, as well as desolation, are such a contradiction to what the spirit is truly about, and its one message of Divine Love.

There are many souls, who are going through a transitional time of letting go of these former teachings and allowing ourselves to get back to our spiritual core and awakening to the possibilities of creating a global community that can live harmoniously, side by side, within the natural laws of the Universe.

So, as we move into the beginning of the 21st century, in a time that we are living now, we find that many people are turning away from the churches and religions, as they no longer bring us the comfort that is necessary to our everyday lives, and most certainly does not provide us with the spirituality that we each, as individuals crave and need in order to find the balance of mind, body and soul.

Unfortunately, by just turning away, does not solve the problem. There is still that void within us, that needs to be nurtured to bring balance back into our lives and allow us to feel whole again. The only way that this void can be alleviated is by exploring and allowing your spiritual self to guide you. Then being spiritual becomes a way of life, and a personal choice of how we choose to live our lives. It is important to remember that Spirituality is not a religion but an integral part of who we are.

As we look around our world today, we see many unfortunate souls who are lost and confused, and do not know where to find the answers, to not only improving and healing their lives but to also finding true happiness from within their soul; and so they search for solutions outside of themselves.

Although we all most probably have similar situations in our lives, which we would like to change, it is not as easy as it sounds, and can often lead to confusion and conflict within, and can sometimes be overwhelming to the point of running around in circles.

To some people, this can even create health difficulties or indeed to some turning to modern-day addictions on a conscious level to help alleviate the deep emotional pain and conflict within.

If the conscious mind is willing to awaken to the spirit within, your soul can help to heal and guide you, on a conscious level, to the path that is right for you.

Your Spirit within, or higher self, is well aware that you have specific purposes within this particular incarnation and also through your spiritual purpose and challenges, that you have agreed to within soul contracts, and always connecting with the Universe to receive that courage, strength and universal love to propel ourselves forward, with the guidance leading you into the environment which is right for you.

You must realise, that we come from a place of Unconditional love, but unfortunately, the environment we are born into today, does not promote this kind of love, kindness and compassion, and therefore life becomes a complete challenge to your soul, who really wants to share and show love, to help others, to be kind and compassionate to each other, and all living beings.

However, in order to survive, in these times, we are only too consciously aware that these type of feelings need to be suppressed, in order to fit in, and to run with the crowd, because the fear of becoming vulnerable, is unthinkable in our present level of understanding, and so with the contradictions of life, conflict with our true self, we find that inner peace is often denied us.

Many people feel incomplete. They know that something needs to change and improve their lives, but they cannot see a way forward with their physical eyes. And yet, still this restlessness within, this drive to move forward continues, and confusion and a feeling of vulnerability and being lost reigns.

You question your values, your purpose, and in some cases, who you are. If this is happening to you, then your spiritual self is urging you to awaken to your higher self, and to become aware of the spirit within, so you can be

7

guided in your path, to understand the Unconditional Love and Energies being directed towards you from the Universe and preparing you to complete your spiritual life purpose, and to find the balance within you to create wellbeing and inner peace.

We come from the Spirit, and we return to the Spirit when this particular incarnation has completed its life purpose and challenges. We are all Spirit in human form, and we are all connected. We are Spiritual Seekers.

CHAPTER 2 THE SPIRITUAL SEEKER

So, who and what is a Spiritual Seeker?   Is this you? Perhaps you have reached a point in your life, where you want to make changes. You are feeling unfulfilled by the life you are currently living, and something inside of you is urging you to explore not only your potential, but to understand who and what you are.

You aim to reach a point of inner peace and balance for yourself and thus allowing you to be happy and satisfied, as is your divine right, and maybe even inspire loved ones around you, to join you in this and perhaps begin to explore their own spiritual journey.

So, you will probably ask yourself, what is my life purpose? Well, most of us want to be happy in our lives, but what will make you happy, truly happy?.

In our society today, we are bombarded with material possessions, that apparently tell us we need to be unique. We are urged to compete with one another to obtain one-upmanship. We are encouraged to suppress our thoughts and true feelings in order to "fit in". We tend to follow a script of behaviour that invisible rules and parameters have risen out of nowhere. We have become so unbalanced within ourselves; there comes the point when we just do not know who we are anymore, or what the future holds for us. Our dreams seem far out of reach, and we seem to be so immersed in the daily functions of life, that we do not have time to stop and question; is this the path to give me what I really need in my life to be completely happy and content.

Truth and honesty have become challenging words, and our true identities are hidden behind our public mask which we have learnt to uphold knowing that kindness, compassion are deemed as a weakness and on the whole, have been replaced with sarcasm, judgements and criticism. This is not true of every soul on the planet, but sadly it does apply to a lot, and these are the people who are lost, as they have accepted society's dictates and forgotten who they indeed are.

This is why, at this moment in our evolution, we must awaken to our spiritual potential, and although as we try to awaken and brighten our energetic light to balance ourselves, we also need to try and inspire the world en-masse, by encouraging those around us, to at least explore their potential as the Universe intended. This is not about converting anyone, but more about inspiring those around you to realise they do have a choice to embellish their life if they would take the time to explore the available opportunities. Everyone has free will which is part of the natural laws of the Universe,

As it stands at this moment in time, it would seem an impossible task, as the world seems to be in constant turmoil. The Universal Law of Free Will is always in play, so therefore we cannot change others, but we can change ourselves.

The only way is for each individual to start to explore from within, and as you find your spiritual purpose and understanding of who you are, there will be some around you, in your life, who will find inspiration from the positive changes in your life, as they have watched you on your journey.

So you could not only inspire them, but perhaps be in a position to help them too, in finding themselves as they begin to take their own spiritual journey. Your choice to become spiritually aware is how it can all begin.

Following a Spiritual way of life is a personal choice as we all have free will, and whichever path we choose to take, our spirit guides will always support and guide you with Universal Unconditional Love guiding you to be the best you can be.

So, we are born into this earth. A spiritual energy, entering into a physical body, to experience a life on Mother Earth, but why?

The quick answer to that question is, our Spirit wishes to live a life in human form, to experience specific challenges, and address any karma, positive and negative, and to inspire others, to fulfil their spiritual life purpose or destiny.

To understand that statement, we have to realise that Mother Earth and its inhabitants are not the beginning and end of life in our Universe, nor indeed the environment we have created for ourselves along the ages. This planet and all its inhabitants, including nature, the elements and the universe as a whole are all linked and meant to work together in peace and harmony for the good of all.

The aim, since time began, has been for humanity to work collectively and harmoniously to create a perfect balance throughout the universe. Rightly or wrongly, we seem to have veered so far off course, that the majority need to awaken to this fact, and contribute to the healing and repairing of this damage.

Unfortunately, we have reached a point in our evolution, where we have severely not only nearly destroyed and damaged Mother Earth and Nature, but Mankind itself, thus having created a cruel world to inhabit. We are all aware this needs to change.

Can we repair this damage and destruction, and bring new growth into our lives? I believe we can, but to bring about this healing, we all need to start to recognise ourselves from within and realise our full potential.

☐

CHAPTER 3 THE POWER OF THE UNIVERSE

We are not alone.

There is, of course, a great deal of speculation on, whether we are the only living beings in the Universe or not. There has always been speculation on parallel universes, as indeed there is also a school of thought, regarding extra-terrestrials, and UFOs.

I can neither confirm nor deny these theories. However, if you look at the magnificence of our universe, and the perfect balance it maintains, it would be rather arrogant to assume it is all for just our benefit.

With the technological era at its height, we now have access to a significant knowledge from the ancient texts, stories and cultures throughout the world, which enables us to widen our vision of who and what we are, as individuals, and as a global community, without the ego-driven guidelines of man that currently insist we live by.

However, whether or not man had help building such things as the pyramids, or whether Atlantis did exist with a race of people with superior intelligence as well as superior technology, are part of a lot of unexplained happenings in our world.

So, whether the ancient civilisations had access to knowledge that we did not, and so much more, is to my mind worth exploring.

We value and judge everything in our lives, by the prominent senses, but what about our intuition, our sixth sense, that inner knowledge that you "know" this is right – why should this not be a logical sense in our everyday life as well. The point is, this is not a "new" sense, but just a sense that we have forgotten how to use.

If we begin to use this sense, in alignment with the others, we could progress by bringing different values into our lives, which would be the first steps towards changing not only our reality but our perspective on our potential and clearing away self-imposed limits.

One thing is for sure, we have only touched the surface of the wonders of the Universe, or maybe even Multiverses, and although Scientists view the world through the eyes of logic, there is so much more information to perceive; if only we would see everything with an open mind, and just as importantly an open heart.

We need to accept that we have the knowledge within us, to shape our lives, with love, kindness and compassion, if we so choose, regardless of who you are, your material wealth, high or low, and your status in this world, because, as you must realise, the spirit within is collectively one, regardless of the physical body it occupies at this time.

We also need to question all information given to us, regardless of the source, until our understanding of said information feels right to us and that we understand it in alignment with our thoughts and beliefs. To put it simply, what does your intuition tell you?

Intuition is a natural feeling. It comes from our emotional chakra, which is primarily the heart. When we reach out from a place of love, we feel good. That is a feeling.

Depending on your emotional State of being, due to your life history, depends how easy or difficult it is for you to access your intuition. Some people, due to the extreme circumstances in their lives, have learnt to shut down their emotions.

If you are a soul that has suffered in this way, not all is lost; you could help yourself by meditating and exploring the self-love pathway. There are also many opportunities to obtain help from like-minded souls. Many therapists practise healing, whether it is Energy healing, reiki healing, acupuncture to Chinese medicine, or homoeopathy to hypnotherapy, whatever is right for you, a helping hand is always available.

The Universe. Where did it all begin? I have asked myself that question, so many times, and yet I am still searching for an answer.

I have listened to many theories, throughout my life, from school, science, religion, philosophies and so much more, and yet although I believe we have some of the answers, I still feel there is so much more missing.

I want to re-examine the evidence we do have, to our history and the wonders of this world, with an open mind and different perspective, as I firmly believe there is a great deal of phenomena and understanding, some of which are, as yet undiscovered, or worse tossed aside as unimportant.

Our understanding of this world, and indeed the Universe, has taken some of us, into our spiritual journey of life and destiny, and yet, to truly explore our individuality and connected potential, it is essential to start our search from within.

In order to begin this journey, we need to awaken to the spiritual soul inside of our physical body, which is begging to be heard and to guide each and every one of us, on our Spiritual Journey to not only bring enlightenment, but to take us into our next step in our spiritual experience encased in this human physical body.

So just how are we connected to the Universe and why?

If you can accept that we are all energy, and that everything is energy and that energy cannot be created or destroyed, you will begin to understand the concept of why we are so much a vital part of the Universe. The concept can be overwhelming.

Everything is Energy, and it is all about vibrations and frequencies. Throughout our history, and indeed even in our present day, there have been pioneers of thoughts and understandings of life beyond as well as within humanity itself. Man, in his arrogance and by definition, his ignorance, believes himself to be superior to the natural world.

So many walk around with a closed mind, drowning in this sea of negativity, that man has created for himself, afraid to look beyond, which is so sad, and yet if they did, their lives would become more beautiful and they could lift their heads, and not only see, but start to live their lives to its full potential.

It is just a matter of change your thoughts and change your reality, but to change your thoughts, you need to change your perspective firstly. Throw away the "learned behaviours" of your past and begin to look at life in a different perspective.

Go within and search through your emotions and allow the love, kindness and compassion reign, instead of hurt, disappointment, injustice and anger. Forgive all those past hurts and suffering. They are gone. It is the memories that cause pain, so forgive them all, and then forgive yourself. By letting go of the pain of memories, you have begun to heal. Then take another look at your thoughts from a new perspective. Allow the love in your heart to look at the world, and its inhabitants, with that love and understanding, and although people and situations still may cause you discomfort or pain, realise they are lashing out at you through their own inner misery and suffering, and instead of hitting back with angry thoughts, send loving energy to heal, and allow the Law of Karma to take effect, which no-one can escape. As you begin to feel the change within yourself, you are not only healing your life, but you are also embarking on a new journey from a different perspective which emanates from within. As your thoughts change, so does your reality.

If only we could see that to live in harmony and peace with not only each other, but in the natural world we live in, it is the only way for man to live and be happy and co-exist. The sad part is, the majority of people, would wish to live their lives in this way, but the environments we live in globally, are very restrictive, but I believe we need to follow our exact evolutionary process, rather than a potential revolution to change the world that we live.

So, do we want to live a life full of anger, rage, frustration, despair, violence? I doubt it. The way mankind has shaped his world, using the tools of nature carelessly, ridiculing the kind-hearted and compassionate souls amongst us, and setting parameters in our lives to prevent us, finding peace and harmony with one another and the planet we occupy, has created a world, where many people are unhappy, not to mention suffering poverty, thirst, disease, and so much more.

This existence is not how it is meant to be. Why should one soul suffer for another's gain, and although the majority do not choose this way of life, it is only by the change of the majority will these harmful ways begin to fade from our existence.

Throughout the centuries, these parameters have created a negative darkness in our world, to the point we are endangering our very own existence. It is time for change.

Needless to say, this is not an easy task, but as in all things, to take that first step, is the prelude to change.

True, we cannot change the world, en-masse, but we can change ourselves, and in time, in my opinion, we could change the world.

CHAPTER 4 OUR SPIRITUAL SELF

If you can look within yourself, and know that you are not content with your life, and I am not talking about your material gains, but the truth of who you are, your inner-peace, harmony as well as the love, kindness and compassion that is in your heart and what is really important to you, and then begin to realise the potential you have within, then you are beginning to learn to align your thoughts to your true spiritual self, thereby creating a more entuned reality for you and yours.

As we open our minds, to what our lives could be like, if we choose to explore, we begin to change our reality. No longer are you held, within your thoughts, by the parameters of the negative darkness. Yes, this can be slower than you would like, and be like baby steps, but you need to think for yourself, as an individual soul, and perhaps begin to understand your life purpose here, as you start to think from within, and this is where guidance from the soul comes in, and I repeat guidance not demands. You, at all times, have free will.

As we start to explore ourselves and who we are, we then begin to awaken to the fact that our potential in this life, is so much more significant than we believed. We then start to take on the concept that we are a spiritual being living a human experience rather than a human being with a spiritual experience.

Once this perspective is reached, your understanding and your exploration of your life, as well as your destiny and potential, take on a much more expansive number of opportunities, and as enlightenment begins, your whole perspective of your life becomes brighter and more colourful.

It is probably true to say, that once this understanding comes into being, that to start your journey, will need you to learn to bring your mind, body and soul into perfect balance, to obtain the gifts that the Universe is trying to give to you.

Abundance is what our lives should be about, and the highest abundance we can attain is pure unconditional love, and as we meet others in our day to day lives, we begin to understand the vibrations of others, attune to them at core level, which is never deceptive, enabling you to look beyond the mask so many of us wear in our daily lives, thus eliminating rash judgements of others, and feeling these vibes will magnetically draw you to and from others on a similar wavelengths.

As we have discussed, our spiritual self is an integral part of our lives in the here now. Once we become aware of our spirituality within, and its role in guiding us throughout our human life, we discover that learning to trust this internal intuition, helps to make us feel complete and we begin to lose that loneliness. This type of isolation is not for people alone; it is more about people who are a close match to your spiritual vibration at this moment in your journey. When we are with others, who understand us, who give and receive willingly, sharing a harmony that we so desperately need, we allow our barriers to come down, and we begin to understand ourselves so much better, and to know there are others who think and feel like we do, brings us courage and strength to explore and attain a more beautiful attunement of spiritual vibration, opening us to the Universe and its energy's that help us to heal our lives and balance ourselves, mind, body and soul.

At this point, we begin to understand where our soul, spirit, higher self, whatever term you choose to use, knows so much more than we do, for our soul is our Sat-Nav for guiding us on our life purpose and journey, knowing that we are a child of the Universe, and that each of our lives have cosmic meaning.

We, as in human form, will never explore our full potential, unless we access our spirit into our human consciousness, and allow ourselves to be guided, with the purity of this Universal Divine love. Understanding this is why undertaking this spiritual journey is not only essential but so beneficial to your well-being.

It amazes me that we are prompted and encouraged by a minority, for their own agenda, and to detach from our own emotions, and not to question why we should give up our individuality to be enslaved with invisible chains. It is our divine right to reach our full potential in this life, and become the best we can be, and fulfil our reason for being. It is, for this reason, why we must grow from a place of love rather than anger.

☐

CHAPTER 5 MIND BODY AND SPIRIT

So, to those of you who wish to begin your spiritual journey, allow me to share with you my own experiences, teachings and spiritual understandings, which I have learnt throughout my life as a Medium, Energy Healer and Spiritual Teacher, and working closely with my Spirit guides from a young age. Hence the reason for this book.

As we have discussed, we are a spiritual being, within a physical body. Our spiritual being works mostly from the heart chakra and guides us with our feelings. We know what we like and love, and when we pay attention to these feelings, we usually choose the right path for ourselves. Our mind, however, is full of logic that has derived from learned behaviours and patterns, and some of these learned behaviours, create an element of fear within us, and prevent us making right decisions and life choices; which our heart is trying to guide us with. I am sure you are familiar with the conflict between head and heart, at certain times in your life.

All the time, the heart and the mind are conflicting, particularly in significant changes in your life, the poor body is so confused and overwhelmed, that sometimes, we can then find ourselves in a state of anxiety, panic and maybe even depression.

Now if you realise, that your spiritual self, holds all the knowledge necessary to guide you through this physical experience, having full understanding of your life purpose, your soul contract(s), your karmic relationships, positive or negative karma to be addressed in this incarnation. Also added to the fact that when you took human form, you do not consciously remember why you have come into this life, or purpose and because of this lack of memory, it becomes part of the lessons we undertake, and how we actually perceive and deal with said challenges, is all part of our spiritual progression, remembering that your spirit is infinite.

Now, with this understanding, it makes perfect sense to listen to our heart, but to do that we need to awaken to the spirit within.

Well, the fact that you are reading this book shows that's something inside of you knows that there is more to life than what you are currently aware. Without a doubt, this is most probably your spirit within urging you towards awakening to the inner voice (*your higher self*) to guide you in a better understanding of who you are, your aims and goals in life. Beginning to give you the courage to speak and understand your truths, and to negate learned behaviours that no longer pertain to who you are today — thus maintaining the balance between your mind body and soul.

To maintain this balance, we have to do an emotional spring clean. As a child, we began to lose those memories of our spiritual life and start to recognise and believe the lessons that we are being taught.

Some of these lessons are essential to our life; some are misguided, some are too general and may not fit our uniqueness, as it is not right to believe "one size fits all" even though the consensus today is precisely that. As unique beings, we cannot be put into boxes to suit the economics of our world. Each person has a uniqueness of natural gifts that should be nurtured rather than suppressed.

Therefore, as we reach out to maturity, our minds are full of learned behaviours. However, some expressions of these learned behaviours create a thought process that can be harmful to us, which is why it is necessary to be aware of who you are and the talents, gifts and potential you and you alone hold.

To balance the mind-body and soul, we need to explore and decide what learned behaviours no longer serve us.

Discarding the learned behaviours that no longer apply in our lives, can sometimes be a difficult journey to take, and when first looking at it, confusion will probably reign, by wondering where to start.

The first place I would suggest you start is to write down all the things that you feel are negative in your life, and then all the things that you think are positive.

When you feel you have completed the lists, address the negativity in your life, and then the positive, and write down how you think you could change it.

It is vital here to look at these negative and positive situations in your life in exquisite detail. It is not a case of "if I win the lottery" I could put this right, and that right as this is speculation, that may or may not happen, and I would remind you here, that we are looking and concentrating on the here and now, in order to change our thoughts and feelings, and by changing our perspective of our lives we then, in effect change our reality.

It is probably true to say that there are certain people in your life currently, who may irritate you or perhaps even make you angry. You will need to examine very closely why they have this effect upon you. Is there a valid reason for their behaviour, and could a different response from you change their behaviour?

To view life from a place of love, within your heart,

22

chakra does give you a fresh perspective of not only your life but your interaction with others.

Ultimately, at the end of the day, when we allow other people's behaviours positive or negative to change the pattern of our life, we are giving our power away.

By giving our power away, consciously or subconsciously, we are lowering our vibrational energy which if prolonged, can manifest in the physical body with the illness or disease.

This is why it is vital to recognise not only who you are, but also your interactions with others. We cannot change other people, but we can change ourselves, and as we change our perspectives, this is where you start to heal your life.

So now we start to shift the balance within us; finally, our heart is invited to join the conversation within. The mind has cleared "Learned behaviours" that no longer serves us, thereby making room for the emotions of the heart to contribute. When we no longer feel restricted in showing our emotions that are true to ourselves, our perspective of ourselves and who we want to be; radiates a strength within that has been waiting to come into being.

As this reality is now being created, your vibration will increase, and your life and opportunities will start to manifest in a much more positive manner. You have begun the healing process.

☐

CHAPTER 6 UNIVERSAL LAWS

As our history books reveal, for many centuries, time has been counted by clock and calendar, and we have lived by Man-made rules and laws.

The Universe also has laws which must be obeyed and understood, but these are born out of love, unlike Man-made laws.

I am not advocating that you, or indeed anybody should break any laws of the society we live in, but I am asking you to include in your life, the laws of the Universe.

As we start to explore the Universe, its laws and our Universal roles in our own lives, we then begin on a path to the abundance we so very much crave in this human existence, and this abundance is first and foremost, Unconditional love for others but just as importantly if not more so, for ourselves.

However, again, in our society, unconditional love is rather difficult to define.

Unconditional love must first and foremost come from your heart chakra, and never be just a learned behaviour. Kindness and compassion in itself promotes unconditional love.

The most natural form of this type of love that we can experience in our lives today is the unconditional love we give to our babies, as they enter into this world, or perhaps a beloved pet that we bring into our heart and home.

We expect nothing in return from either of these, as we consciously realise, they are young and innocent, and we feel not only great joy and pride, but a sense of protecting them, most of all with our love. This is a beautiful example of Unconditional love.

It is when we start to expect something back in return, is where the rules of society, our wants, needs and desires – all born out of learned behaviours – that this love, starts to become complicated and alter our perception of our lives and the people that are in and around us. Suddenly love takes on rules and regulations that go on to include ownership, desires and image – and then distortion of this singular beautiful emotion we are all capable of begins to get ugly.

As these complications appear and our perception of our lives begin to change, our ability to love unconditionally begins to retreat deep within us.

When we start to believe we should have this kind of love, or that kind of love in our lives, because we deserve and need love, it becomes needy; and generally, causes anxiety and can often lead to depression.

When the person/persons, we are directing our love to, is not responding in the way we think they should, regardless of the type of relationship, we begin to question our abilities to be worthy of love.

This is a sure sign that somewhere deep inside of us possibly through learned behaviours, or perhaps someone's offhand comments in our past, has developed an understanding within yourself, that indeed you are not deserving of being loved, because there is something wrong with you.

At this point, this is where the need to explore who you are from within and heal yourself of any external misjudgements that have been held deep within you, to a level that you are not, in this moment, conscious of how they have been driving your thoughts and actions.

As you become aware of this, you will find this is all about your self-esteem. How do you value yourself?

I have often said to my clients, if ten people stood in front of you, and nine of those people told you that you were beautiful/ handsome, but the tenth person said to you that you were ugly, what would you remember and focus upon, and ultimately believe?

You see, irrespective of what others may or may not think of you, the most important person and your evaluation of yourself is what makes you who you are. You do not need approval from an outside source, as you are more than capable of being guided by your own moral compass, in whatever capacity in your life. Deep down, at your spiritual core, you know what is right and what is wrong for you.

When you close out everyone else's opinions of you, and you will likely have to go back to your very early years, and perhaps not only words that were spoken about you, but impressions you received, that led you to believe certain aspects of yourself, and moulded who you are today, and created the negativity you think about yourself, as an adult.

However, if you look deep within yourself, I guarantee that you "know" that you are a good person loving and kind, and by erasing these negative learned behaviours, and knowing who you really are, this will enable you to have the strength and courage to show yourself to the world, and then in this role you will find that you then attract like-minded people into your life, and people in your life who cannot match your new vibrational energy, will step back.

Do not be alarmed at this loss, or have any regrets, because people cross our paths for a reason. Some are temporary, many are permanent, but as in the Tapestry of Life, which we will cover later in this book, everything and everyone has a divine purpose, and so you should have no regrets, but look to see what the lesson has taught you.

Every soul is born innocent and pure, and spiritually speaking we each have a life purpose, soul contracts to maintain and lessons and karmic relationships to endure, for our spiritual progression to be achieved. These are the reasons for each incarnation that our spirit lives through, always hoping to aspire.

Sometimes, in this earthly life, as we meet the challenges of life, some more than others become overwhelming. These challenges are here for a spiritual reason.

When you perceive that these are lessons for us to learn, rather than bad luck, we view these lessons differently, knowing that if presented to us that we do indeed have the answer within us. Again, this is where our spiritual self can guide us in learning these lessons, and then move forward with no regrets.

I might add here, that, we as spiritual beings, before being born into this physical body, we agree to experiencing these contracts and lessons, and very often, it is we, who decide what and who these lessons and karma are going to be in this particular lifetime. So, you see, our spiritual self does indeed know the answers, and we in human form need to learn and trust those answers. When we begin to understand this, we are accessing and using, what is commonly known as our intuition.

The environment and people we are born into, are all part of our character-building process, and as in anything spiritual, it is meant to be.

I suspect you would be surprised to learn that we choose our parents, our siblings and our families to be born into. Nothing is a coincidence. This is the tapestry of life working.

Whatever your family background is, we are all here for a reason. We are here to not only love one another, but also to learn and inspire one another, and if you can appreciate that we each have a role to play in their journeys also, so any negative aspects of this scenario can be turned into positive using spiritual understanding, thereby making more sense in your conscious mind, thus alleviating the need for any guilt feelings. .

As in most situations in life, it is not so much your actions, but your intentions. How you respond to life as it comes towards you, is all part of your learning processes and gives you not only the foundation, but the building blocks of your individual life to complete your life purpose.

We are all aware that life is challenging. It is our intentions that are created from our thoughts that determine how we meet these challenges. So, you see, at the very root of everything, our thoughts are the foundation of our lives. If we can embrace our pure emotions from our hearts, our thoughts will always look for a positive and kind, compassionate conclusion, and irrespective of how the other party(s) respond, you are sitting and living in your truth, thereby enriching your life in the here and now.

☐ .

CHAPTER 7 SELF LOVE

As we begin our spiritual journey, one of the most challenging aspects we encounter is our perception of ourselves. We do not appreciate or value ourselves.

Unfortunately, we tend to look at ourselves with the eyes of the world, but the world does not know us. A common error in this world is that people tend to be put into boxes or categories.

When we realise, that we are each a unique being, and the only accurate assessments of ourselves must come from within; then we can then start to see the personal judgements of the world are not necessary or even valid.

As this realisation comes to us, and we start to look within, we realise there is much more positive and enjoyable aspects about us rather than negative. We can then begin to learn to appreciate our good points and to start to change any negativity we may have. Then upon re-evaluation of ourselves, we begin to see that we have a lot more to give to the world, and ourselves, and that we also deserve Love and respect from others.

Self-love does not mean anything like narcissism or any kind of self-love that has a negative effect on another living being, including oneself.   Self-love is to be happy and content with yourself, without judgement or fear of other's opinion or criticism, of how you are, how you look, or being judged weak because you choose to be kind and compassionate to others. One of the most significant failings today of the human race is judgement, and from these judgements, criticism, sarcasm, bullying and cruelty seem to be the trend.

As you get stronger in your own self-worth, you will realise that this trend is really born out of hurt & pain, and lost souls who have no understanding or awakening of their spiritual core, and as yet, incapable of starting that journey of understanding. So from your spiritual vibration, if you can find it in your heart to send these souls healing love, you will enable yourself to understand that their words really have no meaning and indeed are voiced through ignorance and anger. Obviously, I am not asking you to be a "doormat", but I am asking you to think about your response, its validity to the situation, and why this aggression or violence is being directed at you, and to ask for guidance from the Universe, your Angels, and loved ones in dealing with the situation in hand.

Unconditional love is being who you are and sitting in your own truth of your spiritual self. Allowing your heart to shine its beautiful potential and seeing the beauty and be thankful for it, to embrace the power and wonder of the Universe, which is all part of your birth right, no matter who you are.

CHAPTER 8 IGNITING OUR DIVINE SPARK

As you start to exclude these learned behaviours from within yourself, you are not only raising your vibration, but you are shining your spiritual light for all to see.

Physics states that "energy can neither be created nor destroyed; energy can only be transferred or changed from one form to another."

If you can accept this train of thought, which our scientists in this world, are starting to understand, and hopefully will eventually begin to change their perspective on many areas of our lives on this planet, you can see that we are really so much connected with one another, as well as the Universe, and begin to see the "Divine Spark" that resides in each and every one of us.

As we start to ignite our divine spark and we allow ourselves to live our lives with unconditional love and truth, we begin to realise that this spark has now grown into a beautiful light, that is so bright, that we can now see the potential beauty of our being, and through this within you and your connection with others, as well as nature and Mother Earth, sharing this vibration, the world we live in, could eventually, be healed.

We currently live in a society, globally that is not only troubled, but seems to be immersed in negative darkness, therefore it really is time for us all to connect and shine our light within, by raising our energetic vibration, then we can gradually push away the negative darkness surrounding our planet, and help to heal the world, and mankind, as Mother earth continues on her evolutionary journey. .

I also believe that the Universe has scattered tools

around our planet, to help us in this Evolutionary journey, and that wonders like, Sacred Geometry, and the natural wonders of the world, the oceans, nature itself, as well as philosophers from Ancient times, whose stories are still being spoken of today, are clues to the solutions to the problems we face at this time in our evolution.

These phenomena still need exploration and more importantly, understanding. Man needs to approach this understanding with an open mind and heart.

People themselves, are becoming more caring, as technology, which has its pro's and con's today, does help us to communicate with one another, to join forces to the good of humanity and the planet. We are starting to care about the Oceans and Marine life and doing something good about it – an excellent start to the light shining within these people, and their courage to break from our learned behaviour of "it's not my problem".

These changes, if we look closer can also be observed in many other areas of our lives, and as we begin to question these learned behaviours, and look at them, from a much kinder and compassionate perspective, we find that we are beginning to change our world for the better, and of course, for future generations to come.

When we really take a look at the world around us, and the daily miracles that we see, and very often take for granted, and as you look at the perfection of Mother Earth, nature, the oceans, the planets, and the beauty of it all, why oh why do we abuse it so. All the time Mankind believes in its own supremacy, thereby never willing to relate and blend in with our environment, and instead of looking to merging with nature and the elements, we oppose and aggravate the harmony and perfection of life in every aspect. Until we come from a place of unconditional love, instead of judgement and superiority, to all other living creatures, we will continue on this path of destruction and cruelty that we have found ourselves.

CHAPTER 9 THE LAW OF KARMA

Now we are going to look at the Law of Karma.

Karma is not a judgement. Karma is a result of cause and effect, another of the perfect Universal laws. In our individual lives, when we cause a positive impact, we create positive Karma. Naturally, if we generate an adverse effect, we create a negative Karma.

With the Universal laws in operation, nothing is unseen or forgotten. There is no person, spiritual or human, apart from ourselves, weighing up this Karma.

With this perspective in mind, we can see that when we feel an injustice in play against us, there is no need for any retaliation or revenge, as Karma will balance this out. We may not be privy to witnessing the karmic event, or maybe we will, but to prevent further karmic repercussions, in many cases, if not all, we would do better to defer to the Universal law of Karma.

There are also times in our lives, where we are "attacked" and are forced to go into "defence" mode. This is a time whereby you have every right to defend yourself, but if you try to take the spiritual route in this defence, knowing that Karma is in play for everyone, you are rising above the intentional provocation and releasing yourself from obtaining negative Karma. I am not suggesting that you become a doormat, but to look for the best opportunity for you in any given situation and to be aware of the guidance your spirit within is sending to your heart chakra.

Within this scenario, when we feel we are deliberately provoked, angered, to the point that possibly rage begins to grow, and then the natural step from this is revenge and justification. It is at this stage that taking the spiritual route can be very difficult. Your thoughts will probably create many ideas to wreak vengeance, and although these are mere thoughts to counterbalance the rage and anger, as long as there is no real intention here, this can be overcome. Your thoughts followed by your actions, then becomes cause and effect resulting in Karma. An idea is a thought, because after all, we are still in human form and far from perfect, but a thought or idea, coupled with an intention to action is when cause and effect becomes a reality.

To dissipate the anger, rage and injustice, I would strongly suggest as much Meditation as possible. To connect with your higher self and ask for guidance as well as calmness to appease the anger you are feeling.

Also, to talk it over with someone you trust, a family member or trustworthy friend, or even perhaps a Professional, will always help you to vent your feelings and help you to dilute the negative emotions within.

So, we come into this physical existence, as a Spiritual Energy, a Soul from the Universe, in order to balance any karma we have inherited from past lives, to learn any lessons that we feel we need to learn, in order to spiritually progress, (this can also be karma related) and to work towards our spiritual life purpose that we have chosen to undertake, by taking human form.

In some cases, we want to take human form, to help another soul in their journey, and although we have no physical memory, while in human form, our spirit within has all the necessary knowledge to guide us to complete our journeys.

To understand some of the Law of Karma, I need to touch on the existence of Reincarnation. There are many versions and beliefs on this topic, but I believe, that we are a Spiritual Soul, living many human experiences, to progress Spiritually, to grow and expand our Spiritual Understanding throughout each life, that we choose to live.

We undertake many challenges in human form, all for our spirit to learn and understand and by default, grow and progress. There is always a spiritual purpose and guidance to achieve the purpose.   As I have previously stated, some of these challenges are karmically linked, but not all but the main objective is to face the challenge and learn from the experience in a spiritual way.

Again, I need to remind you that the sole purpose of Spirit, and the Universe, is Unconditional love. There are Spirit Guides and teachers as well as your loved ones, whom you have known and loved in each human experience you have lived, helping to guide you, to complete the reason for your being in this life, to protect you when you are lost or at your lowest ebb, to encourage you in whatever way they can, with no judgement or cruelty but borne out of pure unconditional love, and to try and help you learn that you are not alone, even in your darkest moments.   There are no judgements whatsoever.

There are also Angels, Arch Angels, and of course, the Creator who has many names. In our Western Civilisation Culture, he is called "God", but he is the Divine Source, with a light so pure and intangible, and that we all, regardless of race, creed or colour, are all his children.

Not everybody is ready to awaken to their spiritual self, and because of the Universal law of Free Will, we can only be guided by the Universe and our Spiritual Friends. Life in human form is designed for us to progress, spiritually, and to be the best we can be.

However, as we know, Man has created what I call "learned behaviours" and sometimes Man's inhumanity to Man is more prevalent than it should be.

Although the Spirit Guides, the Universal Energy s all around and within us, unless the spirit which is you within human form, invite them into your life, they can only help to guide you, by inspiring you to follow the right path for your journey, through others, who have invited spirit into their lives.   The North American Indians have a story,

35

which I would like to share with you.

Tale of Two Wolves
An old Cherokee told his grandson,
"My son, there is a battle between two wolves inside us all.
One is Evil. It is anger, jealousy, greed, resentment, inferiority, lies
& ego.
The other is Good. It is joy, peace, love hope, humility, kindness,
empathy & truth."
The boy thought about it, and asked, "Grandfather, which wolf
wins?"
The old man quietly replied, "The one you feed."

Author Unknown.

It is also important to mention here, that we each are born into a human existence, because we choose to, in order to complete a Spiritual life purpose, that will help us grow and expand in our own Souls journey, and in this life, we agree to learn specific lessons, and we choose to meet and be with individual souls, within this human experience, who will teach us, so we can learn lessons, (perhaps even from past mistakes of a previous existence), thus allowing the expansion of our soul to grow.

We choose our parents to be born to, we agree to spend time with different souls, and we continue to remain in this spiral pattern, until we learn the lesson, that we knew we needed to learn for our spiritual progression to continue. These are often called Karmic Relationships, or only Karma.

Karma is a significant Universal Law. I would urge you to remember that Karma is not always negative. Karma has its rewards too. Karma is bringing about balance within your soul.

36

If we choose to visit this lifetime in human form, to address any karma, this is purely our soul's choice, before entering this human form.

CHAPTER 10 THE LAW OF CAUSE AND EFFECT

One of the other relevant Universal Laws, is the law of Cause and Effect. Action and Reaction. We see it everywhere, in our everyday life, but how often do we understand what we are saying and doing.

If you are living your life, unaware of your spiritual self, then the law of Cause and Effect, and ultimately Karma, will take into account, your inability to see how your life choices have a personal effect upon you, and your guides and loved ones, will try to guide you to this awakening and show you that to make better choices in your life, from a spiritual perspective, i.e. kindness, compassion and unconditional love will not only improve your experience, but give you insight into this life in human form, as well as your life purpose and of course, raise your vibrational energy and help you to shine your light for yourself and to inspire others.

We all come into this world, with Spiritual understanding, but as we grow, and are influenced by our environment, people in our lives, we take on these "learned behaviours", and our Spiritual Understanding merges into the background.

As we grow into Adults, and many of us find our lives to be unfulfilled, some to the point of knowing there is a space inside of us, but we do not know where to fill this space, this is usually our Spiritual Self trying to guide us towards seeking the answers to our spiritual awakening, which will not only fill that space within, but guide us to remember our spiritual beginnings in this life, and begin the spiritual journey which is the reason we have taken human form. To once more, find that "inner-child".

Within this understanding we will be guided not only

on our path that is individual to us, but begin in creating a much better reality for ourselves, but also to guide us to people who are meant to cross our paths at certain moments, and whether they be permanent or temporary, each is a challenge and a reward that has been assigned to this lifetime, and is, in fact, part of our destiny.

In our society, our environment and all its expectations of us is very challenging indeed. In many cases, it is challenging to uphold the unconditional love, kindness and compassion that we would like to show in our everyday lives.

It takes courage and strength to standby these emotional commitments of being kind, loving and helpful, and many will jeer and humiliate and be ungrateful for the help you offer.

I implore you not to allow these people and their judgements, criticism and unkindness deter you from being the best you can be. Send them healing energy instead. They are very lost.

We cannot change the world, en-masse, but we can change ourselves. As the old proverb says, with every Acorn, a mighty Oak can grow.

Our world has lost its way. We are out of Sync. There is too much negative energy, and it brings dark vibrations to our world. To counteract this, we must each bring our positive light into being, and as we do, we then raise our vibrations, so that we not only shine a light so bright, others around us, are drawn magnetically to the higher vibrations and can then be inspired by you. Remember though, each of us has free will to choose the path we would like to follow, so you can only try to inspire others, the choice is entirely theirs.

I believe, it is time for the world to wake up and see what damage we are doing, not only to Mother Earth but to all its inhabitants. We can no longer hide our heads in the sand, and we need to evolve and create a reality of goodness and positive energy.

You read about our children being bullied at school, and it takes a tragedy for someone to think, maybe something could have been done.

There are so very many examples, I could quote here, but the crux of the matter is, if we, as individuals, try to live our lives, with kindness and compassion, without judgement, or criticism of others, the law of cause and effect would work in a much more productive way, and create more light, instead of negative darkness.

You are invited to change your action and reactions to come from a place of love, from within using your heart chakra, which meditation can unblock and heal. To come from your Spiritual truths and understanding, and yes in Spiritual truth, you have to take responsibility, and that can sometimes need courage. Here you need to remember you are not alone. The Universe has your back.

You may be in a dark or negative place in your life at the moment, or even feeling trapped and can see no way out of your situation. Your life is your thoughts and your perspective.

You need to let go of any anger and injustices and allow Karma to do its work for you. To search your soul, to find who you are, and what your role in your own life is.

To ground yourself, find balance and inner peace within, to allow yourself freedom from past hurts and emotional turmoil. Meditate as often as you can, daily if possible. Heal your life.

The Universe is trying to give you everything you deserve, and to guide you to a more fulfilled life and emotional fulfilment. Invite the Universe into your life and be guided by the energies they bring you.

This is an example of what it means when you hear people say, change your thoughts and change your life.

You see, your Spirit within you, has the answers you require, and these answers come from your heart, but your mind, which is full of learned behaviours from mankind, does not want you to listen and keeps interrupting you and urging you to take this action or that action, because that is what the world expects of you.

It is time to start to throw away and dispose of the learned behaviours that no longer serve you or the life you wish to live. This is a challenging task to take on, but if you allow your heart to join the conversation within, and allow yourself to "feel" the answers, your thoughts will begin to change. As your thoughts start to change, your perspective alters, and you begin to see a glimmer of light within your own story. Also, if you are smart, you will start to mentally ask your own Spirit Guides and Angels to help you to ignite this light more clearly, so that your pathway begins to unfold.

One word of caution, your mind, which is full of learned behaviours, will try to stifle this, and tell you, you cannot do this or do that, what would other people think, they will laugh at you, they will make you feel foolish and so on. Your mind does not want to let go of these learned behaviours, because it feels powerful and right in its conviction that this is how life should be, because that is what experience has taught it.

A lot of people refer to this mind of learned behaviours, as the Ego, which although right, it always sounds like an abhorrent word to most, but honestly the mind is innocent really, and from birth to toddler remembered its spiritual roots, but as the learned behaviours started to grow, the memory of spirit began to fade, and the learned behaviours took over.

This is why young babies and toddlers are so beautifully innocent and see "imaginary" people, because their link to the Spirit World or Universe is still active.

So you see, we need to go full circle, and retrieve that lost innocence, that "inner child", that was so innocent and bring it forward into our adult lives, which will help us change our thoughts, change our reality and bring us not only inner peace, and balance, but the ability to give and receive unconditional love in our hearts, and realise that love is the only currency of the Universe and Spirit World, which can be ours in the here and now.

☐

CHAPTER 11 - THE LAW OF FREE-WILL

The spiritual understanding of the law of free will, is very complicated to understand, within the confines of our very human existence. I have been a working Medium, Healer and teacher for over forty-five years now, and I, at times, still have difficulty understanding situations where I think to myself, now is this free-will or Gods-will?

By saying "Gods-will" I am referring to the concept of one's destiny, or if you prefer, fate.

Is your destiny set in stone, as it were, or do we have the option of free-will to change or alter it in any way? This is a huge question.

We, as spiritual human beings, really only have "limited free-will". For example, humanity in itself, cannot alter the Sun coming up in the morning, the Moon coming out at night, or the Ocean's, ebbing and flowing with the tides. We cannot change the rotation of the Earth, or the planets as they move through time and space.

So, our free-will comes down to our individuality.

If you look at our free-will from the much broader perspective of the Universe, or maybe even Multiverses, our free-will as individuals, seems minor indeed.

However, as individuals and collectively, we could ultimately change the world we live in, which then positively elevates the collective and then creates a very significant level of vibration, which by the sheer momentum of change, would have a real cause and effect upon mankind and the Universe and our role within its many realms. What a momentous thought!

So, let's go through the opportunities we can explore. We will assume you are not too happy with your life as it is at the moment, on some levels.

You may feel trapped, or blocked in some way, from moving forward in your life. You are experiencing difficulties with one or many aspects of your life, and all

43

you know is that "something needs to change". Well, that's a good start!

Let's be brutally honest here; the grass is never greener on the other side of the street. Nobody has it more comfortable than you, just a different set of problems and difficulties than you have and whatever is in your life, is there for a reason, and either a lesson to be learned or a karma to repay, or perhaps even playing a part in a catalytic event in someone else's journey. Therefore by changing your perspective and understanding of yourself and your reality, the changes you need to make to obtain your happiness and balance and to learn the lesson or complete the karma; is by understanding from a spiritual perspective, which then enables you to make those changes necessary to move forward.

In the world we live in today, in this, the twenty-first century, many believe that the road to happiness is only solved by having an abundance of money.

Money is a commodity that we need and use in this life, whether it is to put food on the table, pay bills, or buy ourselves a Mansion and a fleet of Automobiles. Again, it is a matter of perspective.

When we focus on and love the thought of having an abundance of money, we blinker ourselves, and put all our energies into obtaining said currency. It can even become an obsession for some.

Security is helpful, but is anything material secure? It is also true to say, that what you bring into this life, you take out of – added only by your spiritual experiences by living this life in human form.

So you see, our material possessions, are only temporary, and if we view them as such, rather than giving them all your focus; your perspective on your life, will change and you will start to lift your head and see the beauty in the world around you, and people and living beings that deserve your focus as well.

You then begin creating an abundance of love and

well-being which is so very important to you and especially your heart chakra, and moving you forward, following the path of your life purpose and experiences you have chosen to learn.

Do not think for one moment, that I am intimating that you do not see or care about your loved ones and living beings in and around your life, because I am not.

If anything, I am saying that you are your own worst self-critic, and any negativity in your life, you internally struggle with, is down to your self-worth and your evaluation of yourself.

By exploring who you are, by awakening to your spiritual or higher self, and healing from within, you can make your life so much better, stronger and make choices that are right for you, as your spiritual or higher self knows all what you want in your life, the experiences you wish to explore and the goals you want to achieve, spiritually speaking and when you are listening to this spiritual or higher self, you then find balance and inner peace and a happiness within that no material possession can achieve.

Just think, as we find ourselves, and heal from within, what about our loved ones around us?. Maybe you could inspire them, and perhaps even help them along their spiritual journey, and as we connect with others, we can continue to inspire and learn and grow, and our perspective on life and our world will start to change, and as the light of love shines bright within us, it will be powerful enough to dampen the negative darkness that consumes us, and this world we live in, from negative learned behaviours, patterns and darkness.

CHAPTER 12 - INTENTIONS

As we spiritually awaken and become more aware of the Universal laws; particularly the law of cause and effect, we begin to change our perspective of our thoughts and more importantly, our intentions.

However, when we meet a situation in our life, that we need to act upon, it is our intentions that are important, and your intention can come from a place of what is right under the views of society, or what is right from a place of Unconditional love, and hopefully both.

Whichever way we go through with these intentions or not is irrelevant because unless we view the situation from a place of compassion and love, we are ultimately hurting ourselves.

Thoughts are different to intentions. Yes, we all get moments when we are angry or frustrated, but it is your intentions and action which will denote the damage you may do to yourself, as well as others.

To put it more simply, we are still in human form and have to deal with our lives the best way we can. By having an intention and possibly taking action on that intention will have a cause and effect.

We need to have the right intention and even actions to get the best possible outcome with the least amount of damage or cruelty to anyone even if that means walking away and not seeking revenge or justice thereby allowing the law of karma to resolve the situation in its right time.

By understanding the spiritual value of the Universal Laws, we begin to realise we have no need of the human values of revenge and justice. We also need to remember that this human incarnation is a mere drop in the ocean in respect of our eternal life as a spiritual being. Therefore, the laws of cause and effect, free will and karma balance any kind of injustice and its subsequent ramifications.

I understand completely, the same as you, that actually

understanding and living through the fact that you have no need for justice or revenge, is a challenging task to perform. However, if you struggle with this, ask yourself, does revenge really bring you long term satisfaction and bring you inner peace? I doubt it, because the law of cause and effect can and will create a karmic impact upon yourself. It is difficult in the beginning to understand and therefore trust that the higher power within the Universe will bring balance to the situation in hand, however big or small it may be, but ultimately by trusting this power, you are elevating your own spiritual progress to a place where inner peace can and will be reached.

Again, Karma is not a tool of revenge but rather an extension of the law of cause and effect.

To explain further what I mean by intentions; to me, this is all about hurting yourself. It is not a case of being passive, timid, weak or even cowardly. These are merely words born out of judgements from others, probably again, through learned behaviours and usually accompanied with anger and rage that they have never dealt with.

This is why I urge you to look at your intentions and actions more carefully, so that you do not go out of your way to hurt another living being and if your intention is unable to be actioned upon, in a conducive way, try not to allow the anger or rage, of any injustice take up residence within you, and enable the law of karma to do its job. Remember, your only responsibility is to your soul, and each person living has the same responsibility to his/herself the same as you.

?

CHAPTER 13 – CHAKRA MEDITATION.

Well, we seem to have got to the point of understanding that to change our lives, to bring about self-love and self-healing, then we need to start with the basics, and what better place to start than with our Chakra Meditation. Some of you are probably reading this, and groaning, thinking "oh no, I am not into this!".

I would agree, Meditation is not for everyone, - or so it seems. However, there are many levels of Meditation, and for this, we are going to use a simple, basic lesson in healing ourselves using Chakra Meditation.

As I have said before, everything spiritual comes from within. To obtain Spiritual Awakening we need to access consciously, our spirit within, or higher self, and the best way to attune this energy vibration is to learn how to quieten your mind, and focus within, and to allow the work of access to begin, by clearing, healing and unblocking your Chakra's whilst in a state of Meditative focus.

There are many Chakra's within, which are the gateways to your spiritual soul, or higher self. Like many things in life, when not used regularly, they can become blocked, and dull, and do not function correctly in the designated way. Chi – which is the life force flowing through our bodies, needs to have a clear pathway, so the Chi can flow freely, raising your vibration and giving you a sense and understanding of inner-peace, good energy and well-being.

When this Chi is blocked and forced to make a detour, over some time, it can manifest in ill-health within the physical body.

Back to our learned behaviours, in these modern times, we are urged to exercise our minds, we are also encouraged, to keep our physical bodies fit, but we rarely are called upon to use and apply to our Spirit or Soul.

To obtain balance in our lives, and to raise the vibrations of our Chi, we need to work to find balance between all three, Mind, Body and Spirit.

It is all true to say that people who have had adverse health conditions that using Chakra Meditation daily they have begun to see quite an improvement in their physical health and in some cases significant improvement in even the toughest health issues.

Probably, if we were marketing and advertising the "idea" of Chakra Meditation, the most significant statement to make would be that in a society that is drowning in worry, anxiety and depression, daily Chakra Meditation would seriously decrease these conditions.

You would be surprised just how sophisticated our body intelligence is. If you think of a small cut on your finger. You clean it up, you wait for the bleeding to stop, and then it heals. How does it improve? The body intelligence goes to work to correct the fault, because your mind has accepted that this "cut" is not an acceptable part of your body. This is not merely a case of "mind over matter" but rather a directive from you to heal that part of your body. When your mind, body and spirit are in balance and working as one, the body can correct any imbalances once you choose to recognise them and direct the body to clear away any harmful residues within. Again, positive thoughts of "I am healthy" have a much more positive effect upon your body intelligence, rather than "I am in pain, I hurt, I suffer, and I am sick". Your body intelligence takes its directive from your mind, so a daily mantra of "I am healthy" will set the body intelligence a task to clear away any unwanted and alien activity within you.

I would advocate that each individual tries different versions of Chakra Meditation, until you find the one you are most comfortable with and adapt it to your individual needs. There is a wealth of information on the Internet, as well as many, many books in your library or local bookstores, on this subject.

For this book, however, we are going to talk about simple, basic Chakra Meditation, and learn to begin to get into a daily routine of spending five minutes or so, starting the process of self-healing.

The first Chakra, which is located within, at the base of the spine and is generally so-called

1.   The Root Chakra - This represents our foundation and feeling of being grounded, and when we are walking or surrounded in nature, this Chakra absorbs the energy from Mother Earth, thereby, giving us this grounding feeling thus building the foundation of our Chakra System.

2.   The Sacral Chakra – This is located in the lower abdomen, about two inches below the navel.   This Chakra is connected to our "pleasure" zone, covering our confidence, abundance, new experiences, as well as our desires and sexuality.

3.   The Solar Plexus Chakra – This is located in the upper abdomen, in the stomach area. In this day and age that we are currently living in, time seems to be the thing that is in short supply, and because of the pace we live at, we tend to seriously neglect ourselves and I have noticed in my experiences, the primary situation that seems to cause the most problems for people when they come to me for healing; is the blockage of this Chakra, and it can create a lot of issues to manifest in the physical.

When you look at what the Solar Plexus is aligned to, I am not surprised, and I suspect, neither will you be when you learn that this is the Chakra that controls our self-worth, self-confidence, self-esteem, and how we conduct our lives and view ourselves.

So, it is from our understanding of learned behaviour's,

that we talked about in an earlier chapter, and because of this, we begin to understand that this is where the ego reigns supreme, when allowed the freedom to do so, and because of these conflicts, this is the Chakra that usually needs the most attention.

4. The Heart Chakra - This is found, in the centre of the chest, just above the heart. This chakra controls our ability to love, and when this Chakra is working without any blockages and in good spiritual health, is our most influential and most important connection to our emotions and intuition. When it is blocked or continuously pushed down by us and our environment, it begins to build and build, until moments in our lives can trigger and erupt this emotional volcano, and not only the results but the intense feelings we experience can be so overwhelming. Much like the river, the constant flow is essential to maintain balance, freedom and good "Chi" to keep mind, body and spiritual balance and harmony.

5. The Throat Chakra – This is found in the throat area and is all about our ability to communicate, self-expression of feelings and the truth. This is another essential chakra, particularly in this day and age, as we have learned to suppress our emotions, thus creating an inability to express them. Much like the heart Chakra, we need to express our feelings. Self-expression is essential to well-being and balance. Of course, we cannot go around just saying what we think and feel without thought or feelings of others. However, by Self-expression I really mean, be totally truthful and honest with yourself. Not judgements or behaviours expressed to you by others, but your own self-approval, self-love and self-worthiness. This is all part of the self-healing process.

6. The Third Eye Chakra – This is located on the forehead, between the eyes. Using the third eye chakra, it not only addresses and brings in our intuition, our imagination, our wisdom and our ability to think and make decisions but is an excellent tool in guiding us in the

physical body, on the path that is right for our spirit within.

7. The Crown Chakra – This also is a significant Chakra and located at the top of the head. It gives us our perception of inner and outer beauty, and our connection to spirit and to receive the unconditional love in abundance, creating a state of pure bliss. As you reach the Crown Chakra, having cleared and re-energised the previous ones, your connection to the Universe will be secure, and you will actually feel the intensity of power you now have access to, as is your divine right.

As you begin to see, that if your chakras are blocked or remain inactive with the life force radiating through your body (Chi) they can affect your function and everyday life, and allow all sorts of problems to invade your physical body, and the Chi and your Spiritual Self is not able to function in the way it should, which is to help and guide you, with your life choices, and to journey towards your life purpose and the reasons for this life you are experiencing, bringing you unconditional love and comfort as well as the courage and strength required to face any challenges in front of you.

Once you have reached a point through Chakra Meditation and begin to unblock and heal each Chakra, renewing the energy, and elevating your vibrational energy, you begin to feel a state of well-being, calmness, inner-peace and also an improvement in any current health conditions you may have.

As I talk about raising your vibrations here, this is because energy runs on a frequency, which should be in line with the frequency of Mother Earth, starting with our Root Chakra, and as we raise the vibration within, until we are through to the Crown Chakra, we have reached a level of vibration that is more in-tune with the Universe, and allows us to access the Universal Energy that is in

52

abundance for us to enrich our lives, here on Mother Earth.

If you are feeling lost, perhaps unwell, negative energy, always tired, anxious or maybe even depressed, it is a sure sign that your chakras are lying dormant, attuned to the environment of Man, and its products, and in order to free yourself of these you can begin to turn this around, by focusing on Chakra Meditation, to unblock, cleanse, re-energise and allow your vibrational energy to increase.

Well, let's show you a simple daily routine to, get you started, but as I said before, you can adapt this to whatever way is more comfortable to you.

However you need to make a choice to do this, because you realise you want to raise your vibration whether it is to heal yourself, or give you a sense of inner peace, maybe increase your energy levels, or simply allow yourself to begin the first step of your journey to spiritual awakening, or all of the above – but always, the choice is yours.

Over my many years of working with Spirit, and the people from all walks of life that I have encountered, the main problem seems to be, as I have said before, time.

We run around sometimes, at the speed of light, and everything is rush, rush, rush. That is how life should be, or so we are told. Is that right, though?

Although we all do it, we haven't got time for this or that, and they are all valid reasons, but when do we stop and think just how much damage are we doing to ourselves, because we rarely take time out to take care of ourselves, mind, body and soul. If we do occasionally address all three, we find it hard to focus because going through our minds, is we could be doing this or that. This needs to be a mindset where you feel comfortable and therefore focused on completing this regularly, if not daily, and to be aware not only that this is essential to your wellbeing, but that you deserve it.

We did not come to this physical plane of existence to be rotating on a hamster wheel, and when we are so very exhausted, then we take an enforced rest, and perhaps lucky enough to go on a vacation, which has got to last your body for maybe another few months or longer at a frenetic pace. However, by then you are probably so exhausted and anxious, you will probably need three or four days on that vacation to try to relax enough to enjoy it.

So, this is why I urge you to consciously make an effort to spare yourself five to ten minutes every day to yourself to focus on you, and only you, (bit of self-love here) and go through your Chakra Meditation Routine.

Some are unable to change the pace of their life, to fit in a Chakra Meditation routine without any kind of interruption. This suggestion may help those of you in this situation.

Most of us bathe every day, whether it is Bath or Shower, so why not make your routine to last the duration of your toiletries, where in most cases you are uninterrupted, and can complete it as long or as quickly as suit your needs.

How to complete a Simple Chakra Meditation Routine.

Firstly, make sure you are comfortable and relaxed as you can be. It doesn't matter whether you are lying down on your bed, sofa or even sitting in a chair, or on the floor, or as previously discussed in the bath or shower.

Close your eyes and take three long deep breaths through your nose for four seconds in and then out through your mouth for four seconds. When you have done this, three times start your meditation within.

1. Visualise your ROOT CHAKRA in your mind's eye and think about this Chakra and mentally asking your body intelligence to unblock this Chakra. Breathe nice and slowly throughout and as you finish that sentence, say to your body intelligence, I want you to cleanse, heal and

energise my Root Chakra allowing the Chi to run freely throughout and raise my energetic vibration.

2.   Do precisely the same, visualise your SACRAL CHAKRA, just below your navel, and ask your body intelligence to unblock this Chakra, and then cleanse, heal and energise.

3.   Again, with your SOLAR PLEXUS CHAKRA, in the upper abdomen, the stomach.

4.   Then we move up to the HEART CHAKRA with the same requests.

5.   Again, running up, we voice the same to our THROAT CHAKRA.

6.   Still moving up we go to our THIRD EYE CHAKRA located on our forehead, between our eyes.

7.   And finally, to our CROWN CHAKRA situated at the top of the head, and repeat the same requests and if you so wish, at this point to ask your Spirit Guide, and/or loved ones, and invite them to share your day with you, and guide you to say, do and make the right decisions for you.

As we have discussed, everything is energy. Our Spiritual self is as one, within the physical body that we occupy and indeed animates said body, a little like a driver controls the vehicle's we use in our world today.

As our vibrational energy grows, through our learning of experiences through life, from an infant to maturity, our spiritual body expands beyond the physical, and creates what we call an Auric field, commonly known as the Aura. This Aura vibrates at a much faster rate than our physical body does, and in some respects, it is a representation of the spiritual soul that we are.   It also, interestingly enough, helps to keep the physical body in an upright position from a gravity point of view.

As I have touched on earlier, Auric colours reside at their own frequency, and the colours are reflected from our emotions, from the heart chakra, and our environment that we occupy at any given time, including our thoughts and reality.

Depending where we currently are in our Spiritual evolution, a predominant colour will occupy our Aura and will change vibration as we absorb the current happenings in our life, our environment and most certainly our perspective upon our current location within our spiritual experience.

When we meet another soul, who has a very similar colour and vibration to ourselves, we, on a conscious level "feel" comfortable with that person, even though newly met, and it is because there is a spiritual purpose, why your paths have crossed at this particular time, and that you both have experienced lessons to reach a compatible vibration, to further the journey for both, in whatever capacity, albeit soul contracts, life purpose, karma whichever has been the stronger purpose at this time.

Nothing is a coincidence, and we never meet by chance. This is the Tapestry of Life at work. Everything and everyone has a spiritual reason to this particular part of their journey, which must be in Divine time, and is all part of our life purpose, whether it is just temporary or for an entire lifetime.

The Tapestry of Life does not adhere to any clock or calendar, as the Universe does not count time as we do. The Tapestry of life follows through, as each soul completes a part of their journey, bringing a meeting at the "Divine time" to follow the journey or journeys of all those involved in this particular tapestry of life section. This is often called "Divine Timing" and can often be very difficult to predict in alignment with our clock and calendar, as the soul's journey involved, could take a slight detour, using their free will, before they complete their part of the journey to align with the other soul's journeys involved.

Whether these slight detours are how they are meant to be, within the journey and the Tapestry of Life or not, I do not know. It is true to say, we all have lessons to learn, which is part of our spiritual experiences, and we stay in that pattern until we learn the lesson. Also, on the subject of free-will, or should I say our Limited free will, an example I often use is, "We are in London, and we need to get to Edinburgh.

We could grab a plane ride, or travel by train or car, or even walk the journey, whatever we will reach the destination".

However, if we choose to walk the journey, in respect of our clock and calendar, it is going to take much longer before we can get to our "Divine Timing" moment.

So, the Tapestry of Life continues, and allows us to experience everything we set out to do, as spiritual beings before taking human form.

As we start to understand that our life that we are currently living has so much more purpose than we realise, and the lessons we learn from one another, are all part of the expansion of our Spiritual Soul, which is infinite. It is then, when we reach this understanding, we realise that our perception of life, as we know it, is beautiful in its complexities and resonates within, bringing a sense of inner peace, because we are consciously waking up to our spiritual self, and realise that we are not alone, we are all connected, and our lives have meaning and substance, rather than a constant race to get from one day to the next not fully understanding why we are running towards the future.

CHAPTER 14 – THE TAPESTRY OF LIFE

The Tapestry of Life – Soul Connections

As we have discussed previously, our purpose for this particular life, has already been imprinted within us, ready to guide us through our journey, to people and situations, we are meant to meet, interact with, and to fulfil our spiritual life purpose, karma and learning the lessons we have chosen to experience for the growth of our spiritual self.

Soul contracts are being realised, as we grow and gain the knowledge of understanding, to not only enrich our lives but to also inspire others in their journey.

There are people we feel instantly connected to, even though we consciously think we have met for the first time, and in each, there is a lesson to learn. Do not perceive these lessons to be negative or a chore, because as we move forward in our lives, open-minded to our reality, and the beauty and potential within each one of us, we are continually raising our vibration, and the divine spark which we all hold within, is shining brighter and brighter.

As we magnetically then attract people to us, on a similar vibration, and the spiral continues, we continue to raise our vibrations, and our whole life begins to change for the better.

We then have succeeded in raising ourselves from the negative darkness of learned behaviours, understanding the beauty and potential within us, and as we connect with other beings of a similar vibration the light overshadows the negative darkness of this world and creates a better reality for not only yourself but the people around you and ultimately the whole planet.

It is a fantastic conception, particularly to our human brains, but our Soul within is so much smarter. You soul will always guide you, help you along your journey, and when you are at low points in your life, you will find that your loved ones and your angels draw closer still.

Life throws challenges at us, and sometimes, you cannot see or understand the reasons for this. However, to find balance alongside joy, harmony and abundance in your life, you need positive and negative, to move you along your pathway to meet your destiny.

After all, if you were continually in the light, as it were, you would never recognise the darkness. Understand this, though, darkness does not always mean negativity.

Think about the Sun and the Moon, who each have their functions in our Earth, but life is drawn from the Sun, and beauty is drawn from the Moon, and they complement one another creating a perfect balance. Again, it is your perspective. A child may be scared of the dark, but in the dark, there is beauty. The stars shine bright, in the darkness of night, whereas the view of the child's idea of "monsters under the bed" is a negative perspective. To teach the child to view the beauty of the Stars, instead of the fear of the monsters under the bed, is the better option. Look at the positive and negative in your life, with a new perspective, and make your choices, to obtain the balance that is needed to uplift your life and create a better reality.

When you get to a point in your life, where everything seems to be at loggerheads, and you feel lost and alone and not sure what is the way forward – start to take notice of why the Universe is pushing you out of your comfort zone. There is a reason you are being urged to change things in your life, and as your guides and angels draw closer to bring you love and guidance, you need to look for "signposts" helping you to understand where they are trying to guide you to. Synchronicities are a significant signpost that the Universe and your guides and loved ones, can grab your attention. Signposts or Synchronicities are everywhere, once you understand their significance. Remember also, that they are always loving and guiding you along a path that will be the best for you and your higher self.

☐

CHAPTER 15 - SYNCHRONICITIES

So, what are Synchronicities. Carl Jung, the famous Psychologist, wrote many books and articles about Synchronicities. He also had a strange story about plum pudding to back this up. There is a great deal of literature about Jung's theory or explanation of Universal Synchronicities, but I will let you draw your own conclusions.

However, I will say this, as you know, we are all connected; therefore, telepathic signals or synchronicities come for a reason, as well as the many mysteries that are still unexplored in our generations.

As we begin to understand and apply these synchronicities, we begin to open our eyes to so many possibilities in our life, as well as our potential and connections with other like-minded people.

Remember there are no such things as coincidences and the tapestry of life is the reason for that. It basically supports our understanding of the Tapestry of Life, and that nothing is by chance, and in many ways, we meet and cross paths with other souls, in that divine moment, which has all been previously written for our life purpose, and collectively and held within the core of our spiritual being, which is guiding us towards the completion of our spiritual purpose for living this life.

At specific points in our lives, we sometimes need to take the proverbial right turn, to put us on the right path, to fulfil our spiritual life purpose. Your guides and angels will try to communicate to you, through signposts, impressions, light-bulb moments or simply as Synchronicities, to ask you to be aware that your journey is reaching a significant change. They are asking you to be mindful of your thoughts and ideas, your heart chakra, and what your spiritual self is trying to tell you.

The Universe gives us many forms of signposts, and the more you are open to exploring these signposts and synchronicities, you will begin to learn how to understand and feel the answers you require within. We sometimes refer to this as following your intuition

To understand Universal signposts and synchronicities, you need to accept the fact that there is no such thing as a coincidence. With that in mind, and suddenly there appears to be a coincidence in front of you – change your perspective. What is this trying to tell you. That is a signpost.

There is a song going around in your head. It will not go away. What is the song saying? Who or what does the song remind you of?

You opened a book at a random page, where do your eyes go to first? Does it have significance or bearing on a problem or situation you are trying to resolve?

You keep seeing repeated numbers. On a digital clock, or vehicle number plates, or your eyes are drawn to numbers that seem to resonate within you. What do they mean?

When you start seeing repeated numbers of significant combinations, like 11:11, 22:22, 3:33, these are essential signposts and opening your eyes to some substantial change about to appear along your path.

In the ancient art of Numerology – The Master Numbers are 11 – 22 – 33. There are over a million websites as well as books in plenty, to explore the realms of Numerology.

I am talking more of the Spiritual Understanding of Numerology, as in comparison, the planets do not line up just to give us our daily horoscope. There is so much more to all of this.

I would urge you to explore the Ancient arts, particularly those you feel drawn to, because as we have said, life on this planet, has been guided and created within the Universe since our time began. Throughout our history, there have been souls, in physical form, who have been visionary and have laid down writings in one way or another, to be preserved for discovery when the Universe deems it to be so.

You are being guided along your journey to an improvement in your life, usually a significant development, in order for you to maintain and complete your life purpose, your destiny, and possibly that special someone who you are destined to be with, and this is often associated with the Twin-flame journey, which is a relationship unique in its own right.

Other signposts from the Universe, our loved ones and Spirit Guides, can be finding white feathers around when they shouldn't be there, or perhaps the lights or TV turning on and off, for no apparent reason.

To see a Robin, land in your pathway, or garden, is a strong spiritual message, to take stock of what is happening in your life, and to explore all potential avenues, and allow your thoughts, intuitively to guide you to choose the right path forward.

Complete an intense meditation, and ask to be shown in your mind's eye, the next step forward. Ask for Angelic guidance to assist you in your path. Allow your intuition full reign, and know and feel that whatever you are given, is an indication of your next move in your journey. If you cannot get the full picture on the first go, keep going until you know that it feels right to you. Check and check again, ask for confirmation in any way that is helpful to you. Persevere, and the guidance will come.

Always, always go into meditational guidance with an open mind. Having preconceived ideas of the path, you think you should take will limit your perception of the direction trying to be shown. Clear your mind, deep breathe, and relax and allow your thoughts to drift, and you will begin to see a picture, or memory unfold which is your starting point to receive full guidance on what is ahead for you.

If you are using a Divination tool, like tarot cards, to help you, make sure as you are shuffling the cards, allow your energy to be transferred to the cards, mentally asking for guidance to the questions you are asking. Turn over the cards and carefully allow your eyes to drift to a particular part of the card that you feel drawn to and enable that thought process to wander. Keep going with the cards, and a story will begin to unfold which you will be able to piece together alongside the happenings in your life at the moment. Again, I urge you to be open-minded and no preconceived ideas of the outcome you yearn for.

CHAPTER 16 – SOULMATES, TWIN FLAMES & DIVINE TWIN FLAMES

In today's society, romantic relationships have become so very confusing. Lack of communication, fears of being rejected or alone, not trusting our emotions and in a lot of cases, not sure that you deserve love or happiness.

There are physical, romantic relationships that are just that, and there are physical and spiritual romantic relationships that are stronger, and this is because there is a spiritual connection between two souls.

People everywhere are searching for that soul connection, to feel that unconditional love, to be safe with one another, to not be complicated with any judgement, rejection or suffering, as the soul knows only unconditional love, and when this kind of love is brought into the physical, in a romantic sense, the joining of hearts beats as one.

So why is it so hard to find that Soulmate?

The answer quite simply is, we are drowning in a sea of learned behaviours that tell us the opposite to what our Spirit within knows to be true. When we awaken to our spirit within, and heal ourselves from these learned behaviours, practise self-love and focus on unconditional love, our vibrations change, and we energetically draw our soul mate to us.

The journey towards one another can sometimes be a difficult one, but although challenging, the rewards are blissful. To achieve this state of bliss, both parties need to explore their journey and karma. This is a necessary path to take and learn so that each can reach and be ready for this state of bliss.

For this to happen, you both have to be at a spiritually

vibrational level, that is right for both of you, an energetic match, to continue your journey together.

There are many levels of karmic relationships, and I remind you that karma is just as much about positive as it is about negative, its ultimate purpose is to balance your spiritual account ledger.

There are also many levels of spiritual/physical relationships, and sometimes we have to endure karmic relationships that we begin, sometimes through previous lifetimes, to live through the experience, and finally move on - and by having balanced your karma by completing that relationship, ready to move closer to the real connection that is your destiny in this lifetime.

As I have said, nothing is a coincidence. This is the Tapestry of Life, and the Laws of Karma and Free Will in full play. Soul contracts have to be fulfilled for your spiritual self to progress. If in a previous life, we did not learn the lesson we chose to complete, or in so doing, we caused a negative effect on another soul, and we possibly could have chosen to learn that lesson from a relationship in this life then, to balance the karma and release us from the blockages to enable us to fulfil our life purpose and destiny in this particular life.

These karmic relationships can start out feeling so very right to you, but very quickly small niggles of doubt begin to enter your conscious mind. This, then is a good indication that a karmic relationship is in play. Your spiritual self is asking you to look within, to what karmic lesson needs to be learnt here. Or perhaps, spiritually, you have chosen to spend time with this person, to inspire them to raise their vibration and continue their journey and life purpose. In so doing, you have balanced your karma and able to move forward in your life with no regrets.

So as we go through this life with different romantic relationships, regardless of whether there have been many or few encounters of this nature, if you can realise that each was meant to be, and although perhaps painful at times, you gained insight into yourself, who you are and what you are searching for in your life then you have learnt and are that step closer to your true love and who you were destined to be with. So, no regrets on past relationships, they were for a reason.

The journey towards your true love can be arduous and complicated, and you can look at some couples, who seem to have it all. They meet at a youngish age, they fall in love and stay together blissfully happy – it looks like a dream, as it doesn't seem to happen too often nowadays. Do not be envious of these couples, because spiritually speaking they probably have lived many lifetimes on their soul journey towards one another and finally gone full circle and completed their souls' journey to divine bliss and will be infinitely together, as will you one day.

So, we hear about Soulmates Twin Flames, Twin Rays, Divine Twin Flames and Divine Twin Rays.

The Soulmate journey is not as complicated as the Twin Flame and Divine Twin Flame journey. The difference is, the soulmate journey is about the completion of two souls finding one another and completing their journeys to be together infinitely. The twin's journey is the same but with the added purpose of helping to heal the planet.

To achieve this goal, the twin's need to vibrate at a higher frequency so that when they come together the light within, shines bright at such a magnitude, and with other twins collectively around the planet; this light then pushes the negative darkness in our world, into oblivion. This is why the Twin Flame journey is so challenging, with a Divine spiritual purpose, and you can perhaps understand why the different complexities that the twins experience in this lifetime, is all to achieve that perfect vibration, if you like, to not only find one another in blissful union, but to inspire so many to raise their vibrations, and collectively join the healing of our planet, which is at a time in her evolution that she so needs, to repair and heal the damage, mankind has done in its ignorance.

Before I explain the Twin Flame journey, I have mentioned Divine Twin Flames, and Divine Twin Rays. The journey is very similar in all cases, but the difference between the Rays and the Flames, and the Divine is the vibrational level of the spirit within. These are usually very old souls, who have experienced many lifetimes, and the Rays, have already reached their place in the Spiritual Realms, but have volunteered to return to the Earth's vibration, to help with the healing of our world. As these souls enter into our physical existence and their light is already bright from birth. These people often go into adulthood and become not only Mediums, psychics, healers and Spiritual Teachers, but many humanitarian roles available in our world – but whatever part of the globe they reside in, the vibrational level they emit, will draw people to them, because their goodness within will shine a bright light wherever they go. These people are generally called Lightworkers, and as they walk the earth, people gravitate towards them, and as they do, they cannot help but naturally raise their own vibration and begin to awaken to the potential each of us holds within.

These lightworkers are a Vibrational Magnet, and they are here for a purpose, particularly at this time in our evolution, as it is time that mankind finally learnt the lesson that nature and Mother Earth has been trying to teach us from our very beginnings, that we should all live comfortably side by side with one another, nature and the elements, with love, kindness and compassion allowing our souls to guide us through our individual lives with Unconditional love.

CHAPTER 17 – THE TWIN FLAME JOURNEY

The Twin flame journey is an endurance of the Spirit. It is not a journey for the feint-hearted, neither spiritually nor physically.

The souls that undertake this journey are to be commended. The spirit within is aware of the challenges ahead, and prepares for this, always trying to develop the conscious mind for these challenges. When the conscious mind is awakened to the journey, it feels earth-shattering. There is no conscious understanding of this pairing in our environment, and in many ways, you are not only jumping in the deep end emotionally but fumbling your way through a journey which seems to have no navigation of any degree.

There are times when you feel insanity knocking on your door, and the whole scenario feels bizarre and out of sync with the entire world. Your logical brain, alongside your learned behaviours and understanding of your world at basic material levels, does not make any sense whatsoever, and the separation from your twin, creates a void inside that cannot be fulfilled. Sometimes it feels like an obsession, at best it appears crazy, but if you could stop these feelings you would, because they hurt.

The truth is, your Souls are calling to one another, they are pulling towards one another, and the physical body of each twin, is in a state of flux, because it does not recognise at this point, that the souls are yearning to be reunited as one again. The best course of action if you find yourself in this situation is even though during this time, the two souls will cry out to each other to be reunited, is to focus on yourself. To awaken to your whole spiritual being within the human form, and not only love yourself, forgive yourself and others, clear all negativity from your past and present, and maintain a state of grounding and balance. When you meditate, which I would recommend daily, try to use the Violet Flame, as this is extremely powerful and will help you in so many different levels. The Violet Flame is the most powerful Universal energy for All Flames on their journey.

Even though meeting on the astral while the physical body sleeps, the yearning for permanent reunion is so intense, and that as you become awakened to this journey and accept and surrender to the connection, by offering unconditional love to yourself and your twin, and asking for divine guidance, protection and healing, will the physical reunion, within divine timing be closer to you.

At some point in your journey, you come face to face with your twin, and it is an instant Soul Shock, and then, usually the Runner/Chaser story begins.

One of the twins will be more spiritually aware than the other. This twin is usually the chaser and, in most cases, the feminine soul. The twin who is the runner, often the male counterpart, who runs. They are not running from you, but from the intense emotions they feel, and because they are not as spiritually aware as you, they find it overwhelming and therefore run.

However, as in all things, we can never run away from ourselves, and the Universe is and has been all of your life, working on getting you both to the moment when you can be together, in the right energetic vibration to obtain perfect bliss and to ignite the twin flame, to benefit the planet, as well as yourselves.

You see the twin flame relationship, is one soul, who has been divided into two different bodies. When they meet, in the physical, they are each the other half of the one soul, and mirror one another perfectly, hence the soul shock within the physical body.

However, as we know this path is not an easy one, and the twins have agreed on soul contracts, karma and karmic relationships and a life purpose and to reunite at a particular divine moment to complete the journey together in perfect vibrational bliss,

It is not all bad news though, the good news is there is an energetic connection between them that is so strong, that they can link with one another telepathically, they meet and spend time together in the astral planes whilst their physical body sleeps, and although consciously they are not aware of each other's story, they help one another, with their unconditional love to heal and raise the vibrations drawing their connection together as their journeys progress until that divine moment when they can be together in the physical. In some cases, which is in the minority, they reunite in the spiritual realms rather than in the physical realms, but the connection never breaks, and only grows stronger, but cannot be recognised unless the physical consciousness identifies their spiritual self, and awaken to who they are and their life purpose and their beautiful potential in this lifetime.

The other difficulty which to understand this journey you need to accept, that in the Universe or Spirit, they are not governed by calendar and clock as we are. Twenty, thirty or forty years are mere minutes and seconds to the Universe. The tapestry of life plays a more significant role here also, and so it is as the tapestry comes together that divine moment presents itself.

I know people who have waited Thirty or forty years before they reunite with their twin, but it really is not about the time, but more importantly the lessons we have chosen to learn, the karma and karmic relationships we have decided to balance and the experiences and endurances we have gone through to learn the skills necessary to complete our life purpose, and although in most cases the twin reunion is about romantic love in the physical, it is so much more about unconditional love in the spiritual.

Spiritual teachers in the past would have called these unions, "affinities", but as the new order is coming in to help our whole planet wake up to their spiritual selves, to connect with one another - regardless of race, creed or religion, these twin flames and the light and vibration that they emit, is why we hear of an abundance of them on their journey whereby they will join all the lightworkers in the world, and take us into a much better future where life can be lived harmoniously everywhere, on a higher vibration. That, then is real abundance.

Some people think that this spiritual connection can be broken. I disagree. We know that our whole experience on this planet is for our spiritual growth, and that we at soul core have full knowledge of what we have agreed to experience in this lifetime, and it is our aim to achieve this – so why in physical form, when we have not got these memories, would we try to break a connection that was put in place for a purpose. Far better to explore the opportunities and reasons why this connection is there, what lessons we can learn and to ask for help or guidance from your guides or through a trusted Medium or Spirit Channeller. Very often, by looking at this connection from a different perspective can help you achieve the goal or understand the reason why this connection is there. Shamanic Healing or a Soul Reading can sometimes help, but as in everything, inside of yourself, you do know the answers, and by soul searching and being honest with yourself, will bring you the truth and clarity you desire. Follow your intuition.

CHAPTER 18 – THE AKASHIC RECORDS

The Akashic Record is sometimes called The Book of Life, but I think that a more apt description would be the Book of the Soul.

As we have discussed, we are a Spiritual being, having a series of experiences in human form. We know that we have lived many lives, and the Akashic Record is a mental journal of all our experiences, which are held within us, and we can access fully, when we return to the spiritual realms.

We are also capable, if we so choose, to access these records while still in human form. There are also Mediums and Psychic's, who specialise in Soul Readings, where their Spiritual gifts allow them to access these records on your behalf,

You are also capable yourself to access these, by having as Past Life Regression, with a Past Life Regressionist, or Medium, who could help you to be in a light trance, to obtain a Past Life experience that has some relevance to the current life you are living.

Nothing is lost in the Akashic Records, every thought, feelings, emotions and memories are recorded here, for you to address the balance of your experiences through every human form you have taken, once you return to the Spiritual Realms. This is where we also weigh up our

Karma and begin to address it, to maintain balance at our Spiritual Core.

A great proponent of Akashic Records in the 20th Century, was Edgar Cayce. Cayce had a unique gift, in being able to access people's Akashic Records whether it was past, present or possible futures, to help them in their current lives. He did thousands of readings, in a trance, throughout his lifetime, and subsequently was dubbed "The Sleeping Prophet". There have been many books written about him, and each of his readings were recorded and given a case number, which can be found easily on the Internet.

You can see from a Spiritual point of view, these records are essential, as the Spiritual beings that we are, we choose to experience certain things, in human form, and it is a step by step account of everything we experienced, who we interacted with, our memories, our emotions and thoughts and what we learned from the experience, thus allowing us to progress and serve spiritually.

So how would it help us in current human form, if we do not remember our Spiritual roots?

As we are aware, the Universal natural laws are always in play, and recorded alongside everything else in The Akashic Records.

Perhaps in your current life, you see that you keep repeating a pattern of behaviour, and although you desperately want to change that pattern, you cannot. As that pattern continues to spiral around and around, there is a spiritual lesson to learn here, but you cannot seem to find the answer.

Now, if in one way or another, you accessed, via your Akashic record, a previous experience that had some relevancy to your current life, it might help you to understand what the lesson is, and once understood and acknowledged, enables you to move forward and clear yourself of the pattern.

I really would like to reiterate here; there are no

judgements, only Unconditional love, and our guides, helpers and loved ones are there to serve, guide and help you along your journey within this human form.

☐

CHAPTER 19 - SPIRIT GUIDES

So you are this Spiritual being, and having looked at your Akashic record, you have chosen to take another life in human form, to continue your experiences and spiritual progression, and possibly address any karma, or relationships. You may also decide to make a soul contract(s) with other spiritual beings, who agree to join you in this journey.

Now you need to choose a Spiritual being, to watch over you, guide you and protect you from the point of entering the physical world, throughout until your return. This person is usually known as your Doorkeeper Guide, or sometimes referred to as your Guardian Angel. This person, is often someone you have perhaps had a relationship of some description in a previous incarnation, who agrees quite happily to fulfil this role, to work with you from the Spiritual planes, with pure unconditional love, and fully aware of the experiences you wish to achieve in this life, the positive or negative karma you want to address, and the souls you want to inspire, as well as the soul contracts you have placed into being.

As we know, you then choose who your parents, the family, and environment you will live in, which is all part of the experiences and lessons you want to learn to continue with your Spiritual progression and understanding.

If we are to be born, to remember our Spiritual gifts, to use and help others as Mediums, healers, teachers, humanitarians, we have other guides added to our journey, who are there to teach us, to help others with our abilities, and as we progress in our physical life, the teachers change and new guides and helpers come in, but your doorkeeper

Guide is always constant, and never leaves you.

You are always protected and loved unconditionally by these spiritual beings, who work tirelessly to serve you, and as you awaken to the spirit within, while in human form, you start to feel and sense the presence of this doorkeeper guide, and the memory of that bond that has been forged long ago.

There is a particular prayer that I have always loved, called "Footprints in the Sand" and I think it expresses wonderfully how much we are loved and watched over within that love every step of the way. We are never truly alone.

Footprints in the Sand — Author Unknown

*"One night I dreamed I was walking along
the beach with the Lord,*

*Many scenes from my life flashed across the
sky.*

In each scene, I noticed footprints in the sand.

Sometimes there were two sets of footprints,

Other times there were one set of footprints.

This bothered me because I noticed

77

That during the low periods of my life,

*When I was suffering from anguish, sorrow
or defeat,*

I could see only one set of footprints.

*So I said to the Lord, "You promised me,
Lord, that if I followed you, you would walk
with me always, But I have noticed that
during the most trying periods of my life, there
have only been one set of footprints in the
sand.*

*Why, when I needed you most, you have not
been there for me?"*

*The Lord replied, "The times when you have
seen only one set of footprints, is when I
Carried You."*

Your guides, helpers, teachers and your loved ones who have gone home to the spiritual realms, all have that connection of love for you. As you awaken, within this incarnation, you begin to feel this love surrounding you, and the stronger you connect with your spiritual self, the closer they are to you.

My doorkeeper guide, I found out through a Past Life Regression, was actually my Grandmother in Ancient China, around 210 b.c. called Lady Tan Lu-Chen, but my first experience of spiritual loved ones around me, was my mother, who I lost at the age of 2 years old, but when I was 5, I started to see and hear her around me, talking and loving me, and consequently never felt alone.

As my Mediumistic gifts began to develop, my Lady Tan stepped forward into my life, and the bond between us is lovely today, but I guess I probably owe her quite a few apologies when I return, as I know I have given her a rocky ride in this lifetime, and I thank her, because I know she has a great sense of humour and she is my best friend.

Of course, our loved ones that we have met and loved in this lifetime, are still around us, and although physically they are out of sight, we are always connected very strongly with the love we share, as family, friends or lovers. They usually stay with us, until we can meet again, in the spiritual realms. Where love exists, in whatever form, we will always be reunited when the time is right, including our beloved pets.

On the reverse side of the coin, if there is no love or even a connection between us and someone who has passed over, or someone we felt fear with, whilst in human form, when it is our time to return to the spiritual realms, we will never have to connect, see or hear from that soul ever. The choice is always ours, and the law of free will is still very valid.

When an animal or pet passes to the Spirit world, if that pet has been loved, they will wait with some of your family members, who are lovingly connected to you, until it is your time to be reunited.

If an animal or pet passes to the Spirit world, but is unloved as a pet, they will be welcomed into the group soul.

☐

CHAPTER 20 – MEDIUMS, PSYCHICS & HEALERS

Let's be clear here. We know that we are all spiritual beings within a physical body; therefore, we all have access to the spiritual realms, and information from our loved ones, so by definition, we all have psychic abilities.

I get that this is a wide-spectrum statement, but nevertheless, it is the truth. We, each one of us, has this ability.

As in any gift that has been given to you, you need to fine-tune it, to use it to its full potential. The Psychic is no different from the Singer, the Artist, the Musician, and so many other creative gifts that not only enhance the soul who has the gift, but the outcome for the world at large.

Throughout the centuries, seers, prophets, healers, herbalists, even up to the modern-day psychics and mediums, have been either revered or ridiculed.

By the very act of ridiculing and judging said people, they deny their very own existence and spiritual being, hiding in their physical nature with its ignorance and closed minds.

There is no doubt that people who think this way are coming from a place of learned behaviours, but personally, I think this judgement is more governed by fear than anything else.

Anyone with vision, or what is viewed as far-fetched ideas, seem to be ridiculed today, by too many, and although this is slowly changing, we all need to be much more open-minded to events that could actively be to the good of humanity.

So, let's try and dispel this fear of the unknown.

Obviously, if you are reading this book, you do not hold this fear or disbelief, but I suggest to you that maybe you do know someone, who is of this disposition, and I invite you to try and share your knowledge with them, as it is sad if another human soul is entrenched in the darkness, and too afraid to explore that glimmer of light shining around them, and maybe a helping hand from you releases another soul from that dark place.

Naturally, they have free will, and what they do with this knowledge, is entirely their responsibility, not yours.

There are many levels of development when using your abilities to communicate with our loved ones, guides and teachers in the Spirit World.

Some souls are born with the gifts of Mediumship, healing and teaching of the Spirit.   These are gifts from the Spirit, the same as the Artist, the Singer, the poet, the author, the composer, the list is endless, and each gift has a spiritual purpose that is for the good of humanity.

We all have a role in life, with a particular skillset, and the Mediums, Psychics and Healers are no different. It is with good intentions, from the goodness of their souls, that they try to help people on their journeys through life, knowing that we are all connected, as one from the Universal Divine Source, and we are all working together, at different stages of development, in order to bring man to a point in his evolution of pure love for one another without judgements born out of ignorance, and its associated criticisms and rejections.

If you are a lightworker, and have come to the realisation, that you are actually facing so many challenges in your own life, more so than others, do not despair, as you, with your spiritual co-workers, are expanding your connection in order to be the Spiritual warriors helping to fight the negative darkness that is trying to engulf our planet and its inhabitants. Most Lightworkers throughout time, have had to face the biggest challenges in their lives, as they go through each challenge it strengthens their connection to the spirit world thus enabling them to shed their light on those who are in need.

Many people are often under the illusion that if you

have spiritual gifts and work with them, that you get preferential treatment in your physical life, from the Spirit world, which is not the case, as lightworkers are usually older souls, who have returned in order to serve, and being an old soul, their conviction, knowledge and love of the spirit world, gives them the courage to overcome the challenges set before them.

CHAPTER 21 - SPIRITUAL SYMBOLS

Many people, as they begin to explore their spiritual journey, start to notice so much more around them.

They feel drawn to nature, woods, forests, the sea, rivers, lakes, in fact, the world looks somehow brighter, more colourful.

In this, you are connecting with Mother Earth, and it is grounding you, so that as you open up to your spiritual self, your human form is rooting to nature itself, and the Universal laws as they govern our planet, and you start to notice spiritual symbols, that help you become aware of the spirit people around you.

If you realise that for every soul here, in human form, has a doorkeeper guide, plus loved ones who have passed over, there is a great deal of spiritual activity in and around our planet, not to mention the Angels and Arch-Angels who tend to step in when they can help in an emergency.

I am sure you have heard of people, reliving car accidents and major incidents, where unseen hands have pulled them away from danger or imminent death in the last seconds before doom hit.

If people's free will have created a situation, putting a soul in danger, and it is not that soul's time to return to the spiritual realms, as they have not completed their life purpose, then the Angels and Arch-Angels step in to try to help. Naturally, the Law of Free Will is always in play, and if a soul can be saved, it will be so.

These Spirit folk reside in and around us, but they move at a much faster vibration then we do. They watch over us from a distance, and work with our Auras and the vibration and colours that we emit, and when we ask for them to come closer, or send up a prayer, it is heard within milli-seconds of our time, and they try to guide and help us in any way they can. By asking for their help, or sending a prayer to the divine source, you are inviting them into your life for guidance and assistance, thereby allowing them to step forward without contravening the law of Free-will.

When Mediums and psychics communicate with their spirit guides, in order to give you messages from your loved ones who have passed over, or give you guidance from your own spiritual guides and helpers, the Medium will raise his or her vibration to a faster level, whilst the Medium's spirit guide will slow theirs down, in order to meet somewhere in the middle, for communication to be achieved.

Not all Mediums and Psychics communicate in this way, sometimes they will "read" the Aura, to get messages through and there are some psychics with different "Clair" gifts which enable them to communicate with their guides in different ways.

There are Clairvoyants which is seeing Spirit, Clairaudient which is hearing Spirit and Clairessence, which is feeling spirit, and quite a few other ways. A Medium and Channeller usually allow their guides to put them into what is known as Light Trance and so although you hear the Medium or Channellers own voice, it is often words and information spoken from the Guide.

It is not practised so much today, but some Mediums work with Direct Voice. This is where the Medium is put into a deep trance, and the guide comes through and talks to the audience in the guides voice. There are many instances of this type of mediumship and one of the most significant and well known, is "Silver Birch", who was the Spirit Guide and Teacher of Hanna Swaffer and then Maurice Barbanell.

Again, the literature at information is freely available on the Internet. "The Teachings of Silver Birch" books, available on Amazon and the trance recordings are still available to be read and heard today.

Another is Ivy Northage with her excellent Spirit guide Chan, and their books, as well as Estelle Roberts and her guide Red Cloud.   For those of you interested, these books and audio recordings are well worth reading and listening to.

?

CHAPTER 22 REIKI AND THE ANCIENT HEALING ARTS

Healing is something we are all, at some point in our life, going to need and want to have. Even those who are deemed physically fit. As we have discussed, when the Chakras are blocked or neglected, the Chi, the life force cannot run in a smooth and natural path around our body. With continued neglect, this can, over a considerable period, begin to manifest in physical illness.

To try to improve these physical health issues, Meditation is a beautiful tool to use, and when linked with the Universal Energy which is at your total disposal, this can begin to make great strides in your health, whether it is physical, emotional, or spiritual or even all three.

One of the greatest enemies of good health today is stress. It is impossible to live in a stress-free environment for most people. Continued pressure has a real impact on your health, and to each person, their stress levels reach an all-time high, with certain situations in their life. Nobody escapes. This is where you need to take that leap of faith, and trust in the healing arts to help you alleviate the stress in your life, while you are coping with whatever situation is trying to raise your stress levels and preventing further health issues.

Orthodox medicine does a great job, but it cannot cover everything. If we combine a mixture of Orthodox medicine, alternative treatments and spiritual and energy healing in a combination to suit our own needs, we have a better chance of helping to improve our situation and perhaps even find that we can alleviate all these stresses from our lives and give our mind, body and spirit a better chance of living life in a much better way.

Reiki, as well as Energy Healing, work closely with healing the spirit within, so that your body intelligence can work to making your physical ailments improve.

Reiki is also great for helping stress levels, and of course, daily meditation is a must to find that inner peace within, which by itself not only gives you a more in-depth perspective on your situation in life but allows the stress levels to fade as anxiety and depression are a product of negative energy.

I would suggest, whatever your health issues, try to meditate as often as possible, with asking for health to be restored.   Wake up each day and telling yourself "I am healthy", as you begin to reverse the learned behaviours of being told you are ill.   The body will respond to your instructions of being healthy.   It may take time, but while partaking of one or all of the healing arts, you will begin to become brighter within yourself daily.

Use any or all of the health practitioners at your disposal.   Be happy in your life.   Rejoice in who you are and what you can become. Know that you deserve to be well, balanced and live in harmony.

I am not suggesting there is a miracle cure as such, but with an open mind and an open heart to try some of the healing arts that suit you, your day to day life will be brighter, and of course, the potential is limitless.

CHAPTER 23 - ENERGY VAMPIRES

In your Spiritual Studies, you will come across the term Energy Vampires or perhaps Psychic Vampires. It sounds far worse than it is. Energy Vampires is a term used to describe people who unwittingly draw on your energy and can gradually over time deplete your energy unless you take the correct steps to protect yourself.

This should be done anyway, irrespective of whether you come into contact with Energy Vampires or not

As you are aware, by now, we are all energy and emanating at a vibrational frequency which is in alignment with our spiritual awakening. As we meditate and focus on living our lives, from within our heart chakra, our intuition and third eye chakra begin to resonate at a higher frequency, and we emit a spiritual light, which attracts others of a less high frequency.

For those souls that need healing, particularly emotional healing, will be drawn to your light and vibrations pretty much like a magnet. They are not always consciously aware of this.

They are feeling your spiritual energy, and the warmth and power on a sub-conscious level and feel drawn and want to share your light with you.

This is not a bad thing, as you are in effect, promoting a healing for another soul in need. However, you do need to preserve your own energy and more importantly recharge yourself. This can be done, by plugging into the Universal Energy that surrounds us, and is yours for the taking in abundance.

Let's try to break this down. You, as a spiritual being within human form, know that you would like to help your fellow human souls who are in need.

There is a need within your soul, to help elevate your spiritual progress, and to balance out your spirit within this human form. It is vital to remember here, moderation in everything. Remember, you cannot heal the world all by yourself.

Once you begin to walk the path of the Spirit, you need to acknowledge that you are just as important as the souls you aim to help along your journey.

You will be emotionally sensitive, whether you show this aspect of yourself to the world or not, but it is essential to recognise this part of who you are, and to do everything, with the help of your guides and loved ones, to keep this at optimum levels.

When your emotions are hurt, through the thoughtlessness of other people, this can take a big chunk of our energy, as we begin to make sense of this emotional hurt. You can look at the situation, and see whether this thoughtlessness was intentional or not, and looking at it from all perspectives make the choice that is best for you.

In many cases, the thoughtlessness has derived from lack of knowledge and understanding, and was not deliberate, but it is probably wise for you to take a step back and conserve your energy, asking for the situation to be handed over to the Universe to deal with, which they will do. Remember that you need to ask for their help, so that the Law of Free Will is not contravened in any way.

By taking this action, you are conserving your energies, and helping yourself, and asking for your guides and loved ones to help you to clear the hurt from your energy, and again I reiterate the best form to conserve and protect and recharge your energy is through Meditation.

Daily Meditation is a must when you are trying to help others in the world, and within that Meditation always ask for protection and guidance when dealing with people and situations in your day to day life.

When you are emotionally hurt, try doing an extended meditation perhaps using the Violet Flame as this is a potent Meditation that can create a significant change into our physical lives, whether it is an emotional or physical

89

healing, or to correct the imbalance that has occurred due to pressures within your physical existence.

So, you see Energy Vampires are not really something to be feared, but just ordinary people, who at this moment in time, are at a different level of spiritual and physical understanding then you, and you have probably crossed paths, so that you with your higher frequency, and understanding can give them inspiration to begin their own journey   Just ensure you acknowledge how important you are in this equation and that by merely using your knowledge and understanding, a lot could be achieved here, without energy drainage from yourself.

CHAPTER 24

LAW OF ATTRACTION, MANIFESTING & UNIVERSAL ENERGY

The Law of Attraction, in itself, has been published in so many different ways, that it can become confusing and challenging to manifest on a personal level. The Law of Attraction works, when you understand how finely tuned our lives are, and our individual needs and wants at any given time in our journey. If we focus on something that we think would improve our physical reality, but your spiritual self is aware that by receiving this manifestation, you would be sabotaging your spiritual pathway, then the Universal energy is indeed receiving mixed messages from you.

However, from a Spiritual perspective the Universal Energy is definitely there for us to use, in order to enrich our lives, but in order to maintain the balance we need in a spiritual and physical sense, we have to understand ourselves, in order to ask what is necessary for us in this current life in human form.

We have to take into account, our spiritual life purpose, the challenges and karma we have agreed to receive as well as completing our destiny and aligning with the souls we are meant to meet.

It is not just about tuning your mind to think only positive thoughts; it is so much more. You need to know yourself, at core level, to understand and be guided by your higher self, and once you are aware of where you would really like to be and the environment and people you would like in your life, you can then begin to start to manifest these things into your life, when the divine time is right.

It can be complicated to separate the things we think we want in our lives, and how we believe we can change our environment to achieve those manifestations, but if our higher self knows that these thoughts are incomplete and will not achieve our spiritual purpose in this life, then the Universe will be receiving mixed messages you're your physical consciousness and your higher self, then this will delay you receiving the changes in your life that you are looking for.

This is why, it is so crucial that you first take steps to awaken within to your higher self, and the guidance that is being given to you, and maybe, just maybe the future you see for yourself is much higher and more satisfying than what you had thought for yourself in mere material gains.

The one desire we all want, whether it be physical or spiritual, and that is to be happy and find inner peace.

So, from that starting point, you need to soul search and being extremely honest with yourself, whether or not you think it is possible or not, look at what you think would make you happy and continue to make you happy.

Yes, we are Spirit within human form, but although this life is full of challenges and hardships, we are not meant to be unhappy, or live in just servitude. This is why the Universal Energy is waiting to bring to you the joy you need in your lives to keep you positive, happy and content as you face the challenges in human form that your spirit requires to progress.

Material items are a comfort, but they are not the complete picture. Our emotions, our actual feelings are probably more important. How can you enjoy material gains if you are emotionally unhappy? There needs to be an emotional material balance here. Remember that old saying "Be careful what you wish for, and you just might get it."

Once you awaken to your spiritual self, you will then start to gain glimpses of the way you would like your life to go. This in itself, is a journey – a journey of exploration, and as you begin to learn more about yourself, who you are, at core level, you can start to manifest into your life the tools required to carry you forward.

You will probably know who you are at core level, but I am talking not only a deeper understanding of who you are, but more importantly, an acceptance of who you really are. This will then bring into the surrender of the mind, and its learned behaviours and the freedom of the feelings and guidance from the heart to allow you to resume the journey for the full spiritual and physical potential which is before you.

?

CHAPTER 25- DARK NIGHT OF THE SOUL

The Dark Night of the Soul is not a label that I feel comfortable with, but indeed once we start to explore our Spiritual and Higher self, we do at some point need to surrender to our Spiritual guidance, unconditional love and karmic journeys.

You will most probably come across this term "Dark Night of the Soul" amongst your Spiritual Studies, and you must recognise and ask for the Universe to guide you within this particular part of your journey.

It probably sounds ominous, but in reality, we are clearing the way, for new understanding, spiritual and physical progression by eradicating old thoughts and feelings and possible people and memories of, in your lives, that no longer serve you.

From a physical point of view, this is usually done in some form of isolation. The Universe will aspire to guide you to a place in your life, where you are in some isolation, or surrounded by like-minded people who understand your journey.

Although I am talking about isolation, this is only on a physical level, as your spirit guides, helpers and loved ones never leave you, and will guide, love and support you as you begin to come from this dark tunnel towards the light that is shining ahead, waiting for you to go into your light potential, leaving all negative baggage behind you, no longer attached or affecting you.

The isolation I am talking about does not necessarily have to be a place which is devoid of people, or in some kind of self-imposed prison. It can often mean that you are only surrounded by people that knowingly or unknowingly do not draw of any of your energy and will probably, in fact, give you energetic healing and support through this.

It is possible that before embarking on the journey of the Dark Night of the Soul, you had or have been experiencing symptoms of Depression. However, whichever label we care to use in this instance, obviously the physical body is suffering, and the soul is trying to guide you into a healing of your life, where you are not drowning in negativity. Therefore, experiencing this journey, at the right time, will then allow you to clear negative baggage from your life, and giving your physical body a better sense of wellbeing.

The mind is the vault where these learned behaviours are held. Our heart is where our feelings are. Our emotions and feelings do not lie to us, but our logical mind will very often dispute our emotions and feelings, putting substantial and valid obstacles in the way of you acting upon your feelings.

The mind is full of logic, derived from information received through learned behaviours, environment and people who have taught and set rules of how we should think, feel and live.

The mind is not deliberately misleading us but is making logical decisions on information that can be flawed. Therefore, a correct logical explanation cannot indeed be reached.

However, your heart understands and reads vibes, and this is at a spiritual level, and is also guided by your spiritual higher self. Your heart cannot lie to you, but how you process these feelings with your mind is how you will see it is imperative that the misinformation gathered throughout your years, be vanquished and when you allow your emotions to be the starting point in any decision, your mind will work with you to find not only a spiritual solution but a physical one too.

This journey should not be feared, it is a necessary part

of your evolution, and you are always guided and unconditionally loved throughout. The Universe has your back to put it in simpler terms.

Remember, you always have free-will. It is entirely up to you when and how you start this journey, but I would suggest you look for signs from the Universe, when the time is right for you.

Do you find yourself in an environment where you are isolated from family and friends or surrounded by people of spiritual like-mindedness? Then if you feel ready, take the first step of this journey, knowing you are safe and in good hands. There is no clock or calendar on this journey, and whatever length of time it takes, is entirely in your hands. Don't rush it, take the steps provided, surrender, understand and accept and then take the next level.

CHAPTER 26 – COLOUR ENERGY HEALING

As we are aware, we are energy, and as physics states energy cannot be created or die. Therefore, it stands to reason that our etheric body is not affected by the physical ailments that our body does.

When we awaken to our spiritual self and start to Chakra Meditate, we are continually strengthening the connection and balance of our mind, body and soul,

While our spiritual person has had to remain dormant, it was unable to assist in maintaining good health in the physical – mainly due to the mind shutting it out through learned behaviours.

The spirit cannot intervene until invited to by you and your mind; otherwise, it would be attempting to break one of the Universal laws – namely free will.

Once you begin your Chakra Meditation, you are inviting the spiritual you to blend with your physical body and mind, and as balance begins, a step towards healing the body, the mind and allowing the spiritual you to connect with Divine Universal Energy and the Chi to flow freely throughout your physical body.

The Universal energy that you have access to is immense; in fact, It is infinite.

As you connect to this divine source you can ask for your mind, body and spirit to be at one with the divine source and for you to receive healing to help you with any pain or suffering you might have.

The Universal laws are always in play. Therefore, you must mentally ask for a healing to take place, which is you offering your free will to receive the healing.

In all cases, help and guidance will be given, and even if a health situation cannot be alleviated, because the law of karma is working, then as much relief will be provided, without breaking the Universal laws

So, energy has its own frequency, and at different times in our physical life, our frequency is always changing. Our vibrational energy is reflected in our aura, and the more we understand our own spiritual truths, the expansion of our aura occurs.

The light of that soul reflects through the aura and although it cannot be seen with the physical eyes, it can with the third eye and heart chakra.

Have you ever met someone for the first time and actually "know" they are not only a good person, but someone special and inspiring?

This is because their aura is generating their spiritual self – they are probably an earth angel - and you feel so drawn to them, like a magnet pulling you towards them. You will always feel good around these people because of their pureness of soul, as they are vibrating at a much higher vibration, and when you are in their company, you cannot help but raise your vibration, and you then feel inspired to achieve that frequency for yourself.

You may remember I told you before, that colours have their frequency, therefore if we take our Chakra Meditation a step further and add colours to our meditation, we can manipulate our energy to bring about a healing within ourselves.

The most powerful spiritual colour frequency is the Violet Flame. To visualise oneself within the centre of the Violet Flame and to draw its power within your mind, body and spirit, will bring about a great healing for all and any ailments you may have.

It is also a powerful healing tool, strongly linked to the

Twin Flame journey, and the pain of separation is sometimes so intense on that journey, this Meditation can bring a lot of comfort.

If you research online and in books, you will see many colours associated to each of the seven basic Chakra's, with an excellent explanation of their use.

This is all to the good, however as the Lightworkers around the globe, are raising their vibrations, and indeed nature itself – with many changes that have gone on in recent years, although they have been disastrous, there has been movement, and something positive coming from these occurrences.

We have been experiencing tsunamis, earthquakes, volcanic eruptions, planetary movements, supermoons, and so much more, and Mother Earth as she raises her vibrations, calls on humanity to do the same. This results in the Chakra System in our form, to be increased as we grow and develop.

During your spiritual studies, you will have possibly heard the talk of mankind moving out of Third Dimension into fourth, fifth and even higher dimensions. This is as your spiritual growth within, is allowed by your free will to expand and guide you, to heal you and ground and balance you, and your perception of the world we currently live in, will be brighter, and you can them be aware and see the potential of mankind on earth and work collectively to build it, all from a place of Unconditional Love.

Therefore, I will give you the colours for the primary Seven Chakra's, but as you progress in your meditation, I urge you to allow your spiritual self to show you the colours that are right for you. You will see them through your third eye.

As I have said, each colour has its own frequency, and by allowing your spiritual self to guide you with these colours, you have your own individual frequency that needs fine-tuning, and who better to understand your individuality than you, yourself.

The Root Chakra – the colour here is Red.

This chakra is our grounding and foundational chakra and is very much the one connected to Mother Earth; hence, it is our grounding one. When we worry or get anxious about our survival in our material life, like money, career, bills, food, etc. this chakra can easily be blocked.

Walking in nature often helps this chakra to clear, and if possible, barefooted. To stand still for a few moments, gently stamping our feet, will help with your connection, healing and clearing of blockages.

The Sacral Chakra – the colour here is Orange

This Chakra represents our Sense of Abundance, pleasure, well-being, sexuality.

To maintain a sense of moderation in anything, as over-indulgence again can cause blockages as much as lack of, can. Balance in all things. Chi Meditation, and Yoga can be added to our Chakra Meditation, if needed.

The Solar Plexus Chakra – the colour here is Yellow.

This chakra covers our self-worth, self-esteem and self-confidence.

As an added extra, you could also put on your favourite music, and dance yourself silly. You will be surprised how liberating this is.

The Heart Chakra – the colour here is Green

This Chakra is all about Love, joy, inner peace.

Green coloured foods, and Green Tea can help. The best way for freeing any blockages with this Chakra, is to trust your feelings and open up your heart to other living beings, let the barriers of learned behaviour down, and learn to love and follow your intuition.

The Throat Chakra – the colour here is Blue.

This Chakra is all about Communication and

Expression, particularly of your emotions,

As an added exercise to clear blockages, while you are jigging and dancing around, why not sing at the top of your voice. Wonderful clearance here

The Third Eye Chakra – the colour here is Indigo (a rich deep blue, bordering on Navy)

This Chakra is all about Intuition, imagination, wisdom, and the ability to think and make decisions.

This is where you need to allow your inner child to reign supreme. Enjoy all the magical movies, books and tv shows. Open your mind to the possibility in the belief of a Santa, the leprechauns the fairies, the superhero's, and because they are not real in the sense of fiction and movies, in a way they are. Allow your imagination to roam. Believe in the good again.

The Crown Chakra – the colour here is, yes you guessed it, Violet.

The most potent colour connected to the Universal Energy or Spiritual Realms is Violet, and the more spiritually aware you are, the more powerful this frequency is. Alternative colours here, if you feel you are not ready for the powerful connection with the Violet flame, is that of pure white, gold or silver. These are all powerful frequencies in their own right, and you can try each one until you find the colour that aligns with you at this moment.

This time of Meditation is a bit like charging your mobile phone – in no time you hit 100% charge – pure bliss.

CHAPTER 27 ASTRAL PLANE, NEAR DEATH EXPERIENCES AND PHYSICAL DEATH.

So, what and where is the Astral Plane?

Trust me, I am not a Scientist by any degree, and Mathematics is not my forte. However, I will try to explain about Mother Earth and the Spiritual Realms. This is all about vibrations.

The Universe/Spirit are around us, and they move at a faster vibration and frequency than we do.

There are many levels and realms in Spirit, and as you progress higher, the light is brighter, and the frequency changes as you earn the right to reach the next level. This is why we choose to come back into human form, to gain experiences, lessons, karmic balance, to achieve a higher vibration and to serve man.

A Spiritual Medium, working in human form, (they usually come back to the earth plane, as old souls, to help others with their Mediumistic gifts), and when they communicate with the guides, to give evidence of survival of a loved one who has passed, or healing, they raise their vibration, and the guides lowers their vibration so they can meet and communicate.

As you can see, the Spiritual Realms, the light is pure, bright and perfect. As they come towards the Earth's vibration, unfortunately, it is that much darker, as we seem to be immersed in negative darkness.

The guides train with their own guides and teachers to make the transition from light to dark in order to serve mankind, However, if we in human form, visited our loved ones in Spirit, whilst we are still attached to our human form, we would not be able to cope with the light, therefore there is a place called the Astral Plane, that is like a bridge between the two realms, where we can travel to, in spirit form, whilst our physical body sleeps, still attached to our body with an ethereal cord.

While we sleep, our spiritual self-travels to meet up with our loved ones in Spirit, and lightworkers try to help souls who are in limbo. Twin flames also meet up in the Astral plane to try to heal the connection and the pain of separation in the physical. The only souls we encounter is through a love connection. Regardless of the relationship, in the physical world, if there is love, including pets we have loved, then we can meet on the Astral.

To briefly explain, about Souls in limbo. When we get to the end of our life span in this lifetime, our Spiritual self leaves the physical body by a silver cord, and when this cord is disconnected, the physical body ceases to exist.

You have probably read or heard of Near-Death Experiences (NDE) and people reporting going towards s bright light, which is very accurate, as a few years ago I had an NDE.

However, there are some people, who are adamant in their mind, that when they leave this life, they go nowhere, or to a black hole, and cannot or will not entertain the reality of life after death. In this thought, they are incredibly stubborn and close-minded.

These souls see and feel themselves walking and talking and carrying on with their lives, and they cannot comprehend that they have left their physical presence. It seems illogical to their mind.

They are confused as they are trying to speak to us, but we are not responding, because the majority of people, still living in human form, are not aware of their spiritual senses, and cannot help the soul who is in limbo.

When a lightworker goes to the Astral plane at night, while they sleep; because of their spiritual gifts, and still attached in human form, they are able to bridge the two worlds, and talk to the lost soul to help them over into the light of the spirit world, to be with their loved ones who have gone before. The Universe forgets no soul, and you would be amazed at how many lightworkers work tirelessly to help these souls complete their journey to Spirit.

This is also why, sometimes people feel their homes "haunted" as they sense a presence but cannot communicate with the lost soul, and this is where a Spiritual Medium can help. Remember, nobody is ever forgotten, and even these lost souls, their guides and helpers in the Spiritual realms, call on Mediums and healers in our world to help these people, and they never give up, until that soul has returned to their loved ones in the Spirit world.

CHAPTER 28 – SACRED GEOMETRY

I want to touch briefly onto the subject of Sacred Geometry. When you explore this topic, it makes you realise how much we do not understand about our world.

How amazing the Universe is, in its infinite wisdom, and how the tapestry of life, that is so perfect in its conception, but the understanding is beyond our capabilities, while in human form.

Sacred Geometry describes the geometrical laws which create everything in existence. The geometrical laws derived from the flower of life, produce the blueprint of one consciousness that created life and existence.

The subject we are talking about is vast and worth exploring. It does put an entirely new perspective of how we see the world we live in, and goes back to more or less the beginning of time, and how everything we have built, see and hear has a geometrical pattern that is unique to itself, even to the fact that each snowflake that falls has its own unique design.

There is so much to learn and understand. For instance, how the pyramids were built in such a way that we cannot emulate today, the existence of Atlantis, Metatron's cube, and so it goes on. The Fibonacci Spiral is in nature itself, in fact there is so much to explore and understand, and will make you look at our world, and the Universe, or perhaps even Multi-verses in an entirely different way, and therefore give you an understanding of not only how we are all connected but how perfect the Universe and its laws actually are. I am nowhere near qualified to provide you with actual information on this, but I would urge you to take a look at this subject with an open mind, and as you follow your spiritual understanding, it will help you understand the overwhelming beauty of this earth, and all the occupants, living or otherwise, and how this is all not by chance.

One of the Sacred Geometry tools I would like to look at further is called the Merkabah – and when used in Meditation, can prove to be a potent tool of healing and more importantly a connection to the Universe.

The Merkabah is a gridwork of light and sacred geometry that brings together your physical, spiritual, emotional and mental being. The Merkabah radiates light energy and links you magnetically through your multidimensional self with the infinite Universe. Exploring this meditation, strengthens your connection to the Universe, helping you to manifest abundance in your life. By Abundance, I mean happiness, joy, love, well-being as well as the material item's you need to be happy and content. You can manifest what you are ready to receive in this divine moment. Spirit Science have made a movie on Sacred Geometry and can be found on places like YouTube as well as Spirit Science's own website.

https://spiritsciencecentral.com/spirit-science/full-episode-list/sacred-geometry-movie/

Taking a look at this may help you to understand the subject a little better.

CHAPTER 29 – SO YOUR JOURNEY HAS BEGUN

So you have reached a point in your life, where you are ready to explore who you are, and what role you want to play in your own life. By following the path to your destiny, you will begin to feel not only at peace with yourself, but to know that there are many opportunities for you to discover.

As I have repeatedly said, throughout this book – your journey must first and foremost start with you.

You have probably had many trials and tribulations in your life, and some emotional, and even possibly physical damage has occurred.

No-one can change the past, but we can improve our perspective of it.

First, have no regrets.

Whatever happened in your life, was for a reason. What did you learn? Did your situation help and inspire another soul or souls? Did something good come out of it? Did you remember the positive as well as the negative? Finally, can you forgive those involved and far more importantly, can you forgive yourself?

When you realise, that your spiritual being has agreed for some reason or another to endure and learn from these challenges, you understand in the physical sense, that you did not make the wrong decision. You have no need to feel guilty or perhaps humiliated that you allowed it to happen to you, and that actually it may have been a blessing in disguise, as in the physical being, you learned from it, and from a spiritual point of view, you completed your mission to experience these situations and further your spiritual progression.

Karma, from previous existences was probably addressed and balanced, in not only yourself but if any other souls who were involved too, therefore the tapestry of life has been allowed to move forward.

So, when looking back in your life, with spiritual eyes, it is easy to forgive your human self, and put the past behind you.

When you have dealt with your past, and it does take time, but trust me when I say take your time, and deal with it by calling on your spiritual strength, your guides, helpers and loved ones in spirit, and perhaps even a close trusted friend, or someone who has understanding of the spiritual way of life. Seek knowledge of this nature, wherever you can, and if that knowledge makes sense to you and it feels right, then accept it. If, however, you are given insight that you cannot accept at this time, then put it to one side, until you are ready to understand.

So, here we are – in the here and now. You have looked back and resolved issues, and you are now free.

You probably feel lighter in yourself, not so burdened, but possibly a bit shaky as this is a whole new beginning. One you are eager to explore, but still a bit wary as to what to expect.

Take your time. By clearing the past, you have raised your spiritual vibration. The frequency you are expelling at the moment, the physical body is a little unused to, and you need to allow it to settle and sync the vibrations of the spirit within the physical body. Be kind to yourself here. Listen to your body, if it tells you its tired, then rest. You find yourself craving certain foods, then have them, follow your instincts. Don't overindulge, everything in moderation, because what we are doing here, is self-healing.

You may even feel like going into isolation mode, and that is good for a while, but again, everything in moderation.

Naturally, life goes on, and so you have to merge "being good to yourself" with your "lifestyle", but truthfully, if you can keep the mindset of being kind to yourself rather than beating yourself up, this goes a long way into healing yourself.

So, now we come into the present time in your journey. We have started to awaken to our spiritual self, and now we need to strengthen that awakening, and we need to look at all our learned behaviours and clear ourselves of those, that no longer serve us.

As you take a different and spiritual perspective of your life, and your reason for living this life, the path ahead becomes more exciting and not so lonely.

Your intuition seems to be more grounded and dependable, and you are listening with your heart and allowing your true nature to come through, without the shackles of man-made judgements and criticisms. You are beginning to sit in your own truth and better still, you are starting to get to know who you really are.

With this insight, ideas and dreams come back into your life; you start to reactivate the inner child, you smile more, you are not so anxious, you are becoming whole again.

As you develop and grow, your light shines brighter, people around you respond differently to you, in a much more positive way – and as your thoughts change, your reality changes too. Opportunities that were not there before start to arrive You meet new people in your life, and they are more in tune with you, as you are with them, as your vibration continues to increase. Your perspective on your life is continuously changing and getting stronger, and the material security that was once so very important, has also taken up a different view in your life, and with it the anxiety and stress that you were drowning in has certainly lessened, if not disappeared and you are now coming from a place of Unconditional love.

Chakra Meditation walks in nature or by the sea, or possibly both. Talking with like-minded people, enjoying your loved ones and family, and do not be afraid to show kindness and compassion to other living beings. All this will bring more abundance into your life, and you will inspire others as your light within gets brighter and brighter, and somewhere in this journey, you will find your dreams manifesting into your reality. The Universe is waiting to reward you, but until you can know and love yourself, only then will you know what to ask for,

Enjoy your life. Explore your potential. Inspire others and be Inspired yourself, because that is who we are meant to be. Love and Light.

Copyright © 2019 Sylvia Knell
All rights reserved.
ISBN: 9781704686097

Printed in Poland
by Amazon Fulfillment
Poland Sp. z o.o., Wrocław

38983328R00063